Team Foundation Server 2012 Starter

Your quick start guide to TFS 2012, top features, and best practices with hands on examples

Jakob Ehn

Terje Sandstrøm

[PACKT] PUBLISHING enterprise

professional expertise distilled

BIRMINGHAM - MUMBAI

Team Foundation Server 2012 Starter

First published: November 2012

Production Reference: 1161112

Published by Packt Publishing Ltd.
Livery Place
35 Livery Street
Birmingham B3 2PB, UK.

ISBN 978-1-84968-838-3

www.packtpub.com

Credits

Authors

Jakob Ehn

Terje Sandstrøm

Reviewer

Mathias Olausson

Acquisition Editor

Edward Bowkett

Commissioning Editor

Meeta Rajani

Technical Editor

Lubna Shaikh

Project Coordinator

Michelle Quadros

Proofreader

Mario Cecere

Graphics

Aditi Gajjar

Production Coordinator

Prachali Bhiwandkar

Cover Work

Prachali Bhiwandkar

Cover Work

Conidon Miranda

About the authors

Jakob Ehn is currently a Microsoft Visual Studio ALM MVP and also a Visual Studio ALM Ranger. Jakob has 15 years experience in the IT industry, and currently works as a solution architect at Inmeta Crayon ASA, specializing in Visual Studio ALM.

He actively participates in the MSDN forums and contributes to different open source projects, such as the Community TFS Build Extensions and the Community TFS Build Manager.

Jakob's blog: `http://geekswithblogs.net/Jakob`

Jakob's Twitter: **@JakobEhn**

Terje Sandstrøm is a Microsoft Visual Studio ALM MVP for four years. He works as Chief Software Architect at Inmeta Crayon ASA, specializing in Visual Studio ALM.

He loves the community, works with the Community TFS Build Extensions, participates in the forums, and has free extensions uploaded to the Visual Studio Gallery.

More about Terje: `http://about.me/TerjeS`

Terje's blog: `http://geekswithblogs.net/Terje`

Terje's Twitter: `@OsirisTerje`

About the reviewer

Mathias Olausson works as the ALM practice lead for Transcendent Group, specializing in software craftsmanship and application lifecycle management. With over 15 years experience as a software consultant and trainer, he has worked in numerous projects and organizations, which have been very valuable when using Visual Studio as a tool for improving the way we build software. Olausson has been a Microsoft Visual Studio ALM MVP for four years. He is also active as a Visual Studio ALM Ranger, most recently in the role of Project Lead for the Visual Studio Lab Management Guide project. Olausson is a frequent speaker on Visual Studio and Team Foundation Server at conferences and industry events, and blogs at `http://msmvps.com/blogs/molausson`.

He has worked on *Pro Application Lifecycle Management with Visual Studio 2012* (*APress, 1430243449*), which can be found at `http://www.amazon.com/Application-Lifecycle-Management-Visual-Professional/dp/1430243449/`.

www.PacktPub.com

Support files, eBooks, discount offers and more

You might want to visit www.PacktPub.com for support files and downloads related to your book.

Did you know that Packt offers eBook versions of every book published, with PDF and ePub files available? You can upgrade to the eBook version at www.PacktPub.com and as a print book customer, you are entitled to a discount on the eBook copy. Get in touch with us at service@packtpub.com for more details.

At www.PacktPub.com, you can also read a collection of free technical articles, sign up for a range of free newsletters and receive exclusive discounts and offers on Packt books and eBooks.

Instant Updates on New Packt Books

Get notified! Find out when new books are published by following @PacktEnterprise on Twitter, or the *Packt Enterprise* Facebook page.

Table of Contents

Team Foundation Server 2012 Starter

Welcome to the Team Foundation Server 2012 Starter. This book has been especially created to provide you with all the information that you need to speed with **Team Foundation Server 2012** (**TFS 2012**). You will learn how to set up TFS 2012, get started with version control, work items, continuous build and manual functional testing, and learn some best practices and useful tricks of the trade. You will also learn to access the TFS from other tools including Excel, and utilize the Web Access for those roles who don't use Visual Studio as their daily tool.

This document contains the following sections:

So what is TFS 2012? – find out what TFS 2012 actually is, what you can do with it, see common scenarios for use, and why it's so great.

Installing TFS 2012 – this section shows the different upfront choices regarding the adaption of TFS 2012 to your organization that you have to make, how to install it in different setups, and how to configure it for maximum benefits

The section covers:

- Local install
- On-premises single server setup
- TFS Services (Azure) setup

Quick start – after installing TFS 2012, learn how to quickly get started with your first project. This section covers:

- Creating a new Team Project with the appropriate process template
- Creating a product backlog and planning a sprint
- Adding a solution to source control
- Creating a Continuous Integration build

Top features you need to know about – TFS 2012 is more of a platform than a fixed product. It can be configured, adapted, and extended to match your needs to a very high degree. This section will cover the use of the fundamental features of TFS 2012, which do not require any adaption. You will learn about the following:

- *Version control* – the following topics will be covered here:
    - The fundamentals of TFS 2012 version control, using changesets, checkins, and history
    - Retrieving code from any version, annotation, labels, and so on.
    - How to structure your source code according to best practices and plan for future branching
    - How to branch and merge your code
    - Migration from Visual Source Safe
- *Work items* – the following topics will be covered here:
    - The fundamental work items types and how to use them
    - Creating work items
    - Querying work items
    - Transferring work items to other tools, such as Excel
- *The Agile workbench* – the following topics will be covered here:
    - How to use the new Agile Workbench
    - Setting up teams and areas
    - Planning iterations
    - Using the backlog
    - Using the task board

- *Build* – the following topics will be covered here:
    - You can't live without the TFS Build! Here you learn how to use it!
    - Setting up a minimum build system
    - Configuring a Continuous Integration build for your solution
    - Monitoring builds
- *Functional test* – the following topics will be covered here:
    - How to do functional testing—manually or automated
    - Setting up a test plan
    - Performing a test run
    - Doing exploratory testing

People and places you should get to know – in this day and age, it is impossible to live without the Internet and it is here that you can find resources as well as help for your possible TFS 2012 woes. This section provides you with many useful links to the project pages and forums, as well as a number of helpful articles, tutorials, blogs, and the Twitter feeds of TFS 2012 super-contributors.

So, what is Team Foundation Server 2012?

Team Foundation Server 2012 (**TFS 2012**) is the latest version of Microsoft's **Application Lifecycle Management** (**ALM**) system. It covers all the aspects of managing a software product over its complete lifecycle, from inception, through development and the subsequent maintenance phase for as long as it is in use.

TFS 2012 governs all the aspects of software development, including requirement management, project management, development, testing, deployment and quality assurance. It has four major traits that make this very valuable:

- Traceability
- Visibility
- Automation
- Flexibility

An important aspect is the multiple ways of accessing TFS 2012. It can be accessed using the brilliantly new Agile Web Access, using Visual Studio, or a multitude of other development IDEs, Microsoft Office products, or even through Java development platforms such as Eclipse. There is also a rich ecosystem of third-party tools available, which integrates into TFS 2012. Some examples include inteGREAT from eDevTech, TeamCompanion from Ekobit, and InRelease from InCycle Software.

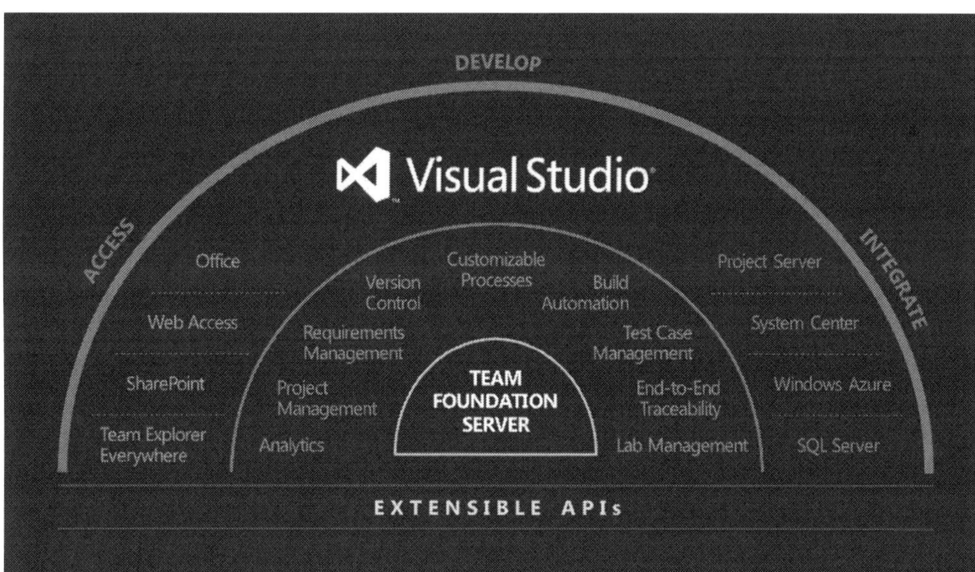

TFS 2012 has four major operational parts or stores, namely the work item system, the version control system, the build system, and the test system. In addition, it has a reporting data warehouse and a SharePoint project portal; the latter can be used for both document management and for accessing reports. It is a multi-role system, so that all the major roles in an organization can use TFS 2012 for their own purpose.

TFS 2012's major advantage lies in its internal integration. All the stores are coupled together so that information is automatically linked together as the different operations take place.

A typical case story for how different roles work together using TFS 2012 is as follows:

1. A Stakeholder adds a requirement to the work item system using the Agile Web Access.
2. An Architect sits down with the stakeholder and enters test cases as the acceptance criteria into the work item system using the test manager, and in doing so, connects the requirements with the test cases.
3. The Product Owner moves the requirements into the upcoming sprint.
4. The Scrum Master sits down with the team and breaks down the requirement in tasks using Excel.
5. The Developer receives the task in Visual Studio and develops the source code. He/she checks in the source code to the version control system of TFS 2012, and in doing so connects the task work item with that source code.
6. The TFS 2012 build system detects the check in and starts an automated build. The build is connected to both the source code and the task work item.
7. The tester detects a new build in his test manager, and starts running a new test run based on the test cases entered earlier and the compiled code based on the new build.
8. A Bug is detected, and the Test Runner collects information from the Test System with all its Test Results, connects this to the bug, and the bug to the test case and the build.

The circle is now complete—all these artifacts are all stored in TFS 2012 and what is so great—the artifacts are all linked together! Anyone can now access this information from any point, and drill down into any other part of connected items.

This story showed a scenario with many roles and many processes in place, but you can start much simpler. You can even start without nearly anything. For example just start with testing, run an **exploratory test session** with nothing else in place; just run the test and create bugs as you find them. From there you can, if you like, use the bugs to create test cases, and collect the test cases together to form user stories.

These are just some examples of the flexibility you have. TFS 2012 can support nearly any process you have, and you can choose for yourself how much or how little you want to use. Then, as time goes on, you can add more features, without compromising anything you have done earlier.

Installation

TFS 2012 can be installed in multiple ways. We will cover the most common ones, which are as follows:

- **Basic installation**: This is an install on any local computer you have, and installs on Windows 7, Windows 8, or any of the server operating systems from Windows Server 2008 and upwards. It's a great way to try out TFS, but can be used in production for single developers or small teams, and is covered under the TFS Express license.

  The Basic installation gives you Source Control, Work Items, Build automation, and Test Management. There is no Data warehouse, reports, or SharePoint portals included.
- **Standard/advanced installation**: The solution for larger companies is the server installs or Advanced configurations. There are multiple ways to configure this, and we will cover a fundamental single server install with the build server separately.
- **Team Foundation Service**: This is the hosted version of TFS. You only need to sign up to the service. The offering is currently free, but Microsoft will charge for this service at some time in the future.

Option A – Basic installation

Basic installation is well suited when you want to try out the core functionality of TFS. You can install and configure **TFS Basic** on your local machine in less than ten minutes.

Step 1 – Running the setup

Start by running the installation (`Setup.exe`) from the TFS installation media. The installation itself just installs all the binaries; it doesn't require you to configure anything. It will install the .NET 4.5 Framework, which might require a machine restart as part of the installation.

The interesting things happen afterwards when you run the **Configuration Center**. This wizard launches automatically and lets you choose what kind of installation of TFS 2012 you want.

Step 2 – Configuration

In the **Configuration Center** window, select the **Basic** option and press the **Start Wizard** button. On the **Welcome** page that follows, press **Next**.

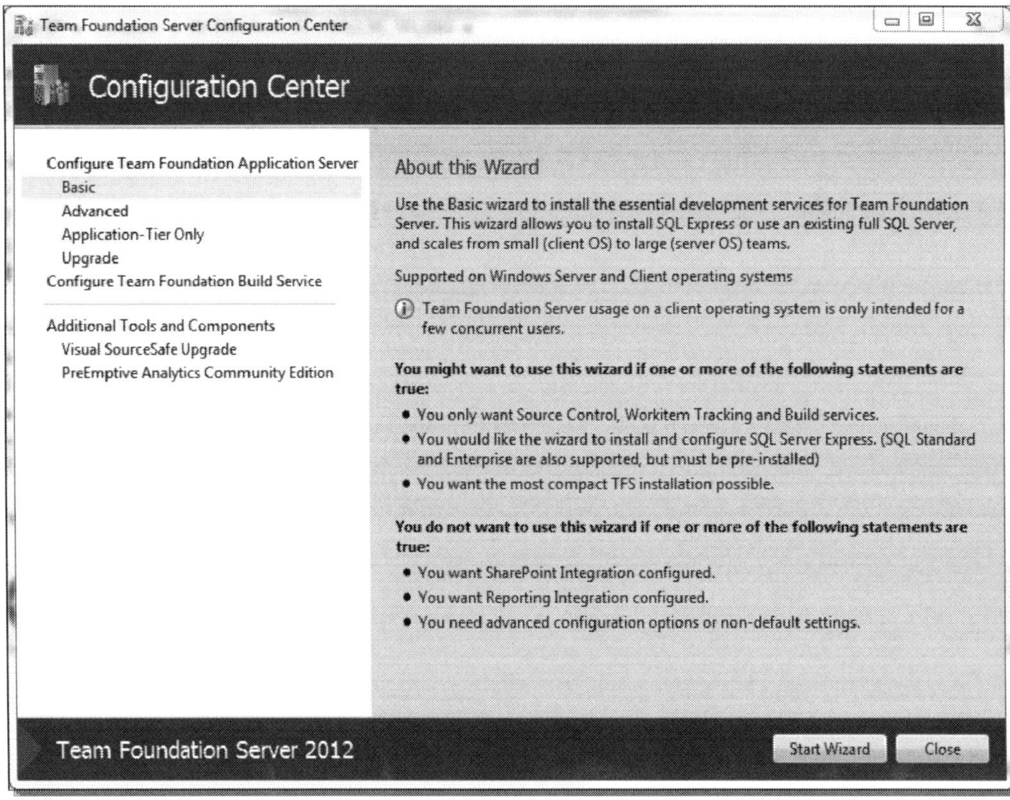

Step 3 – Setting up the database

Now, you need to choose which database server you want to use. You have the following two options:

- Let TFS install SQL 2012 Express for you
- Point to an existing SQL Server instance, which must be SQL 2008 R2 or SQL Server 2012

If you already have an existing SQL Express instance on your machine, then the first option is disabled, as shown in the following screenshot:

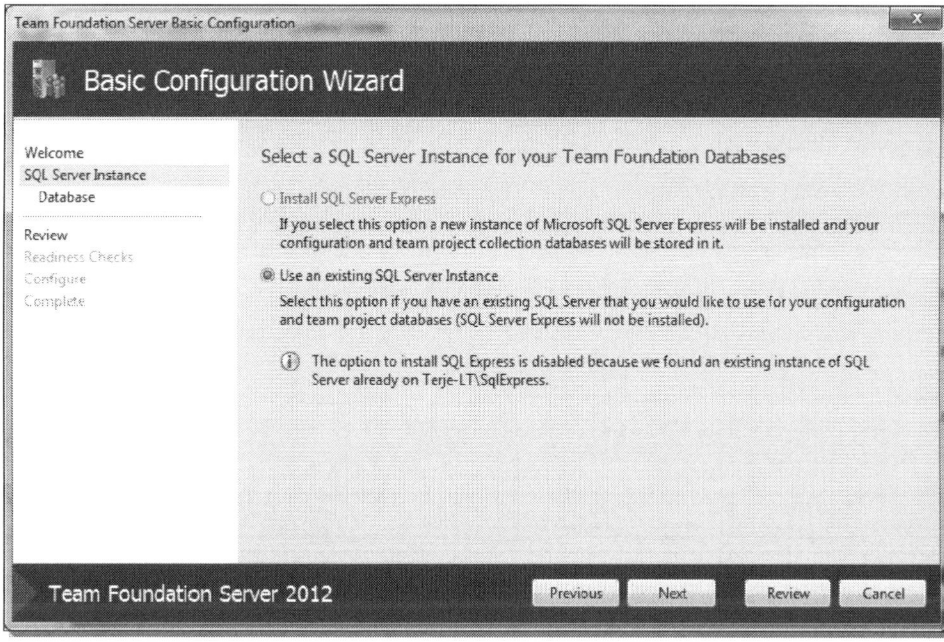

If you do point to an existing SQL instance, then you need to supply a name for **SQL Server Instance**. Note that the SQL server must be located on the same machine; the Basic installation does not support remote SQL servers.

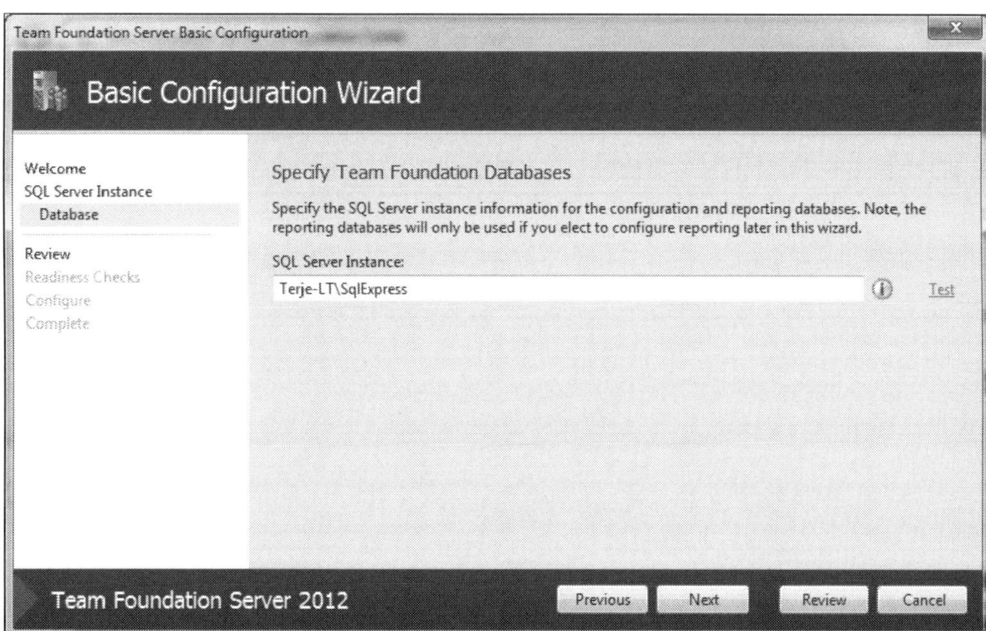

Also note that if the existing SQL instance Express is not a SQL 2012 Express instance, then it will be automatically upgraded to SQL 2012 Express. However, if your installation is not at least SQL 2008 SP2 Express, then you will be asked to upgrade to that level first.

Step 4 – Reviewing

The next page will run through a set of review steps, making sure that everything is configured correctly. If any errors are shown here, you need to correct them and then you can re-run the reviews. Press **Next** to start the configuration.

Step 5 – Performing the configuration

Now, the configuration wizard will perform the configuration to complete the installation of TFS 2012:

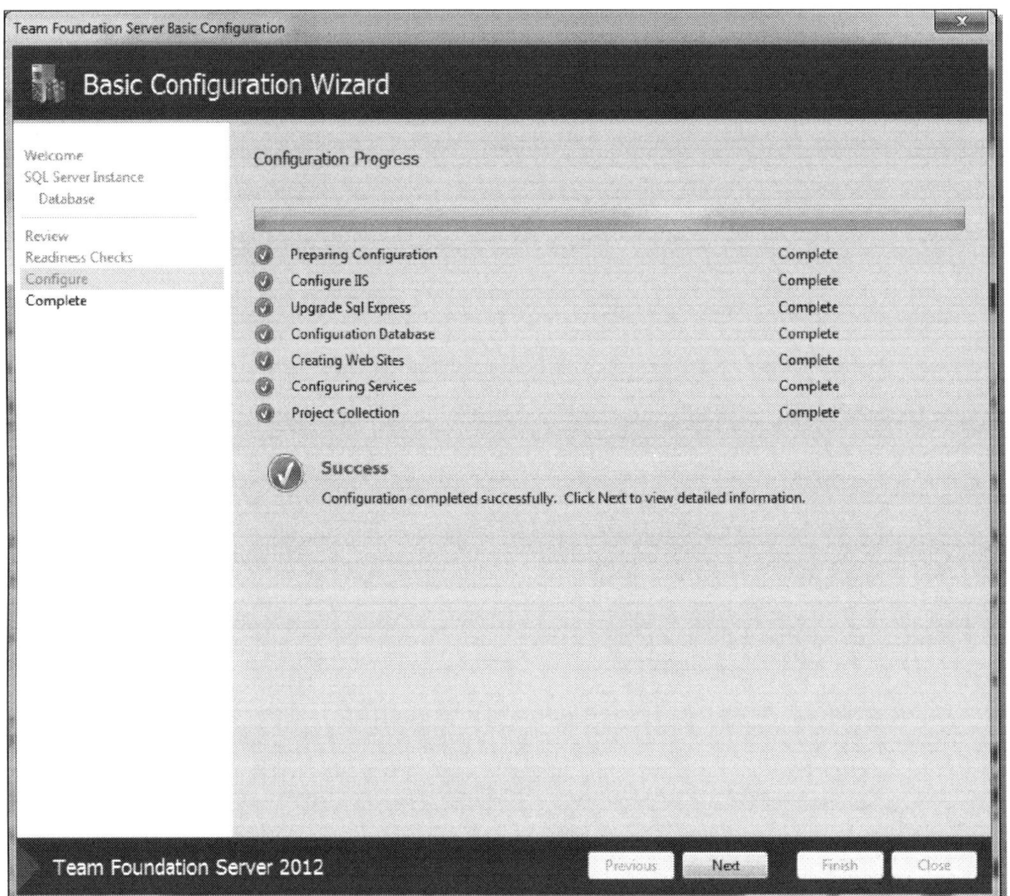

That's it

The installation is now complete. The information shown on the final screen includes the URL, which all users will use for connection, and some information about what changes were made by the configuration wizard on external resources, such as IIS and the Firewall:

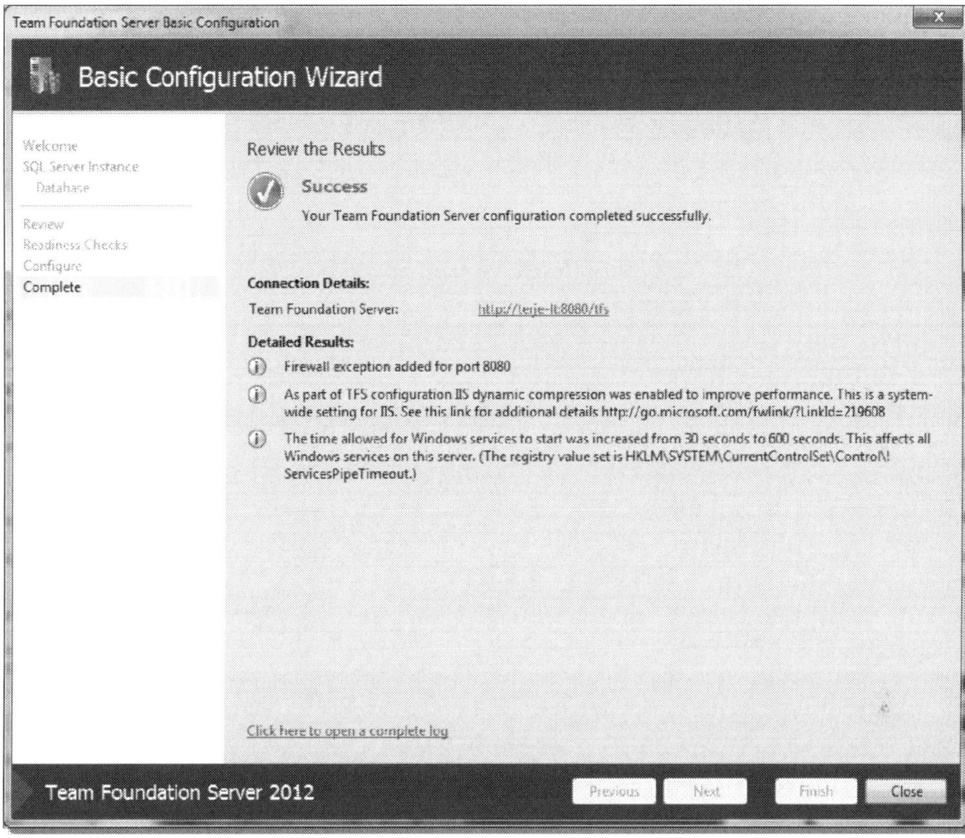

You are now ready to start using TFS 2012! Check out the *Quick Start* section for how to quickly get started on a new project.

Option B – Standard server installation

For the production server, a full TFS server install should be used. This includes, in addition to the core TFS components, SQL Reporting Services for the reports, SQL Analysis Services for the data warehouse, and Windows SharePoint Foundation for the team project portals. When using the **Standard installation** option, everything will be installed on the same machine. If you need to scale out your TFS installation from the beginning (for example, by using a separate server for the data tier) then you must choose the **Advanced installation** option. Note that you can always scale out your deployment later.

The Standard installation and configuration has three main differences compared to the Basic installation:

- You need to supply a Windows account that is used as the service account for SharePoint Products and for the read-only account, for accessing the SQL Server Reporting Services reports. It does not need to have any special permission; a normal workgroup/domain user is enough:

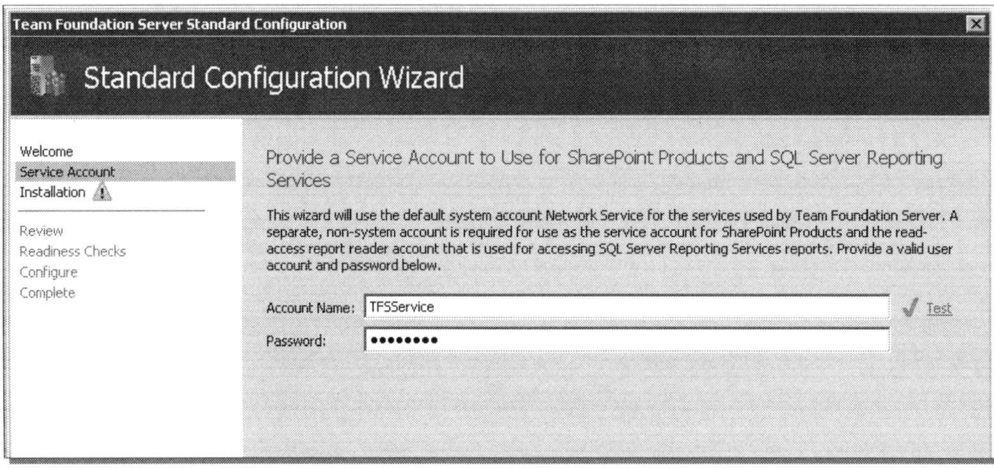

- SQL Server will not be installed; there must be a SQL Server running on the machine before you configure the TFS installation. Note that the SQL Server must have been installed with both SQL Reporting Services and SQL Analysis Services.
- The Standard installation option will install Microsoft SharePoint Foundation 2010 as part of the installation process, unless already installed:

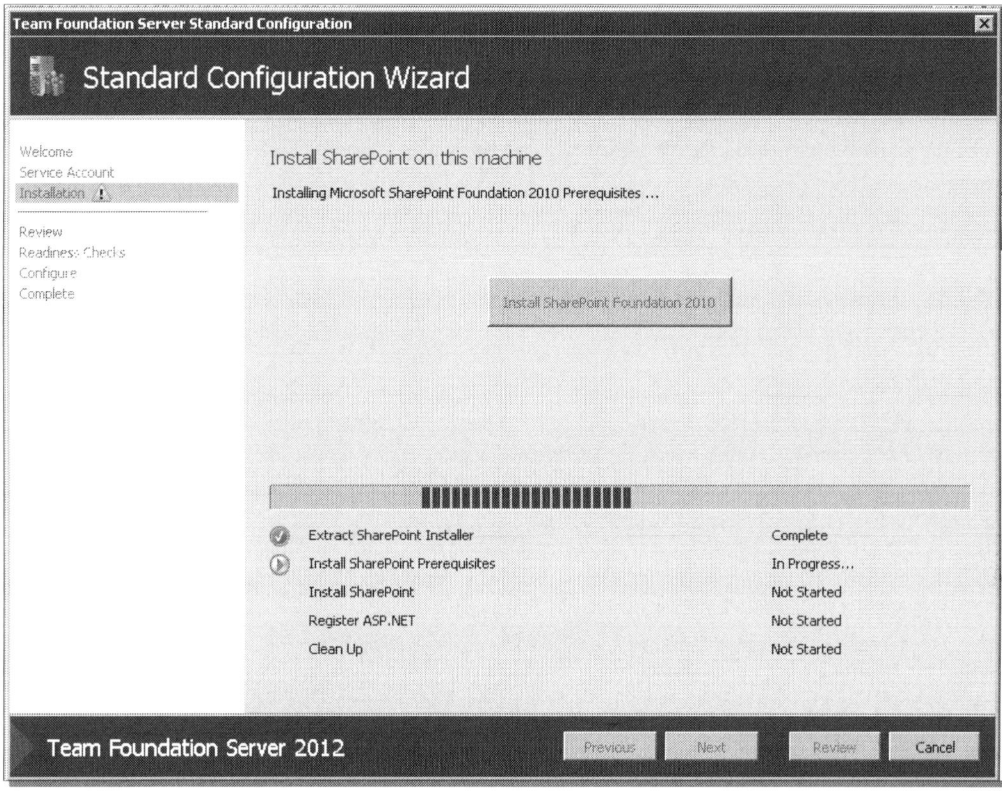

Option C – Team Foundation Service

Another great option, not only for quickly trying out TFS but also for use in production, is the hosted version of TFS. This is TFS running in Windows Azure. Team Foundation Service fully supports Source Control, Work Items, Test Management, and Build Automation. It does not (currently) include support for data warehouse, reports, and a SharePoint portal.

Step 1 – What do I need

All you need to sign up to TFS Service is a Live ID account. If you don't have one, sign up at `https://signup.live.com`.

Step 2 – Signing up to the TFS service

1. Go to `http://tfs.visualstudio.com`, and click on the **get started for free** link:

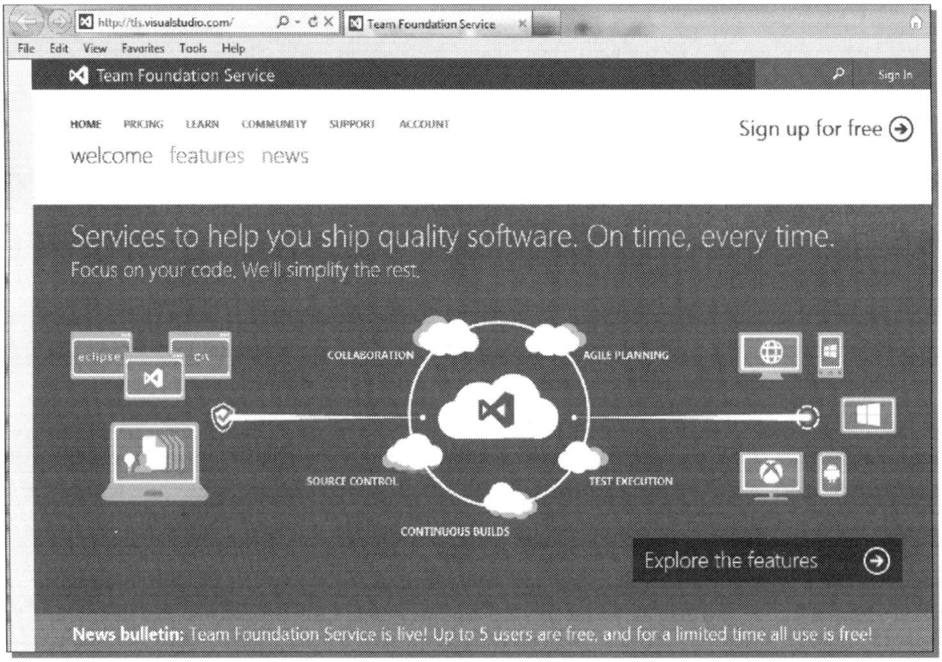

2. Create your TFS account using your Live ID:

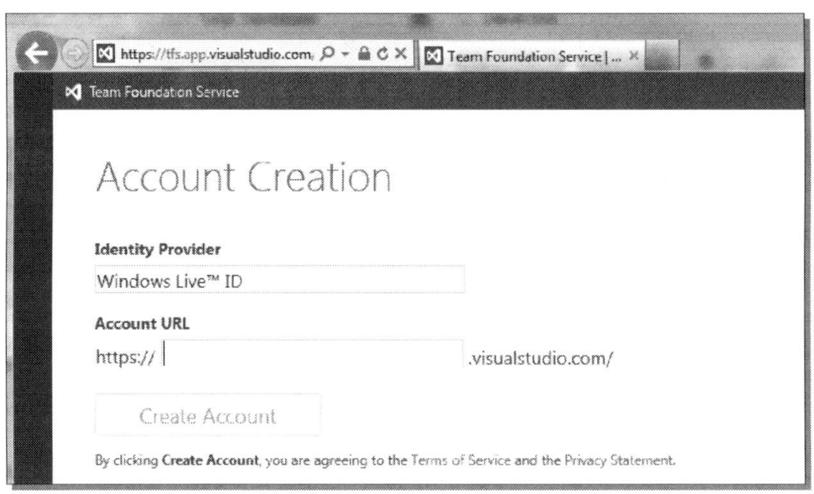

There is currently only the Windows Live ID identity provider that works for TFS Service, so leave this screen as it is.

Quick start – Creating your first project

In this chapter, we will walk through a sample project and, using that as an example, work through the different steps that you need to do to get this into the TFS 2012, including setting up the team project, adding requirements, using the source control, and setting up a build.

We will use the fictional **Packt Diner restaurant** as the sample project. The restaurant needs an application for its waiters, to help them automate the order processing and payment. This application will be called `WaiterApp`. We will have two developers on the team, `Jakob` and `Terje`, and a project owner, `Meeta`.

Step 1 – Finding and connecting to the TFS 2012

We will connect from our client machine to a TFS 2012 server using Visual Studio or the Web Access.

1. When you installed TFS2012, you were given a URL to the instance.If you don't remember it, open up **Team Foundation Server Administration Console,** found under **All Programs/Microsoft Visual Studio Team Foundation Server 2012** on the machine where you installed the server:

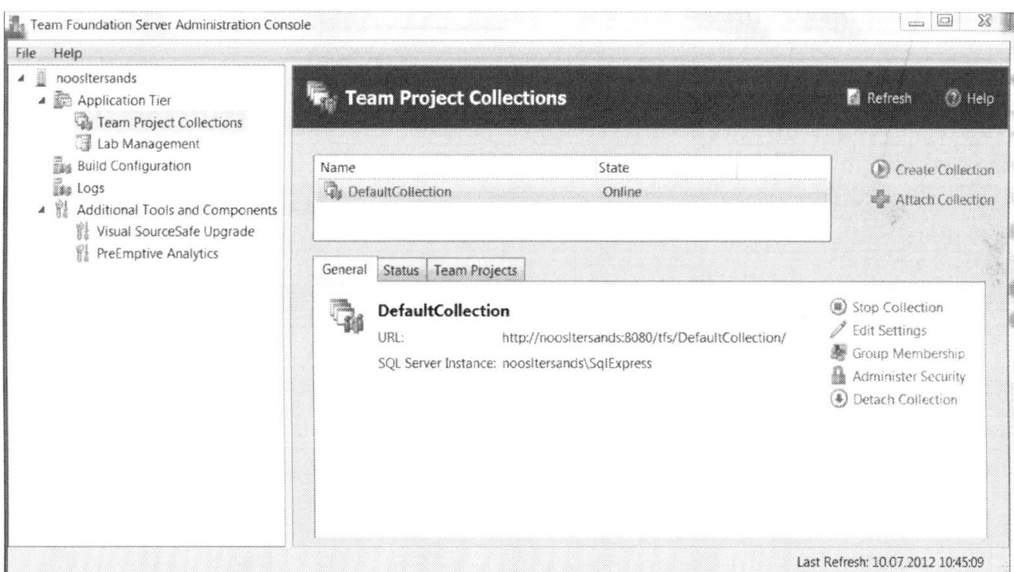

2. Select the **Team Project Collections** under **Application Tier**, and notice the URL for **DefaultCollection**. It will look similar to the previous screenshot, except that the first name will be the name of your computer (name of the computer on which you installed TFS 2012 on).

3. Back in Visual Studio, locate the **Team** menu, and select **Connect to Team Foundation Server**.
4. The **Select the Team Foundation Server** list will be empty, so press the **Add Servers** button.
5. In the **Add/Remove Server** dialog box, the list will be empty. So press the **Add** button.
6. In the **Add** dialog box, enter the computer name (found in step 2) in the **Name or URL of Team Foundation Server** field. Leave the other fields as they are by default. Verify that the URL that gets displayed in **Preview** field must match the one found in step 2. Also notice that you can paste in a complete URL in the first field.

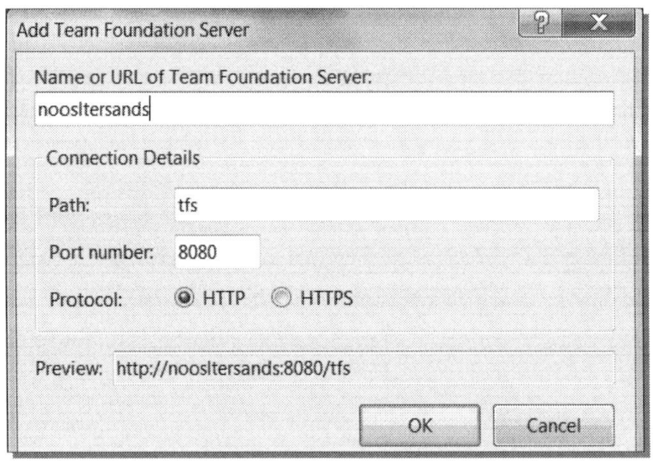

7. Accept by pressing the **OK** button. A confirmation dialog will then pop up; accept that. You will now see the connection dialog box. Press the **Connect** button.

You have now connected Visual Studio to the TFS 2012 instance.

Step 2 – Creating a team project

A **Team Project** is a TFS 2012 organizational term that provides isolation. It can represent many things, but in this case we will let it represent the Packt Diner restaurant. The restaurant may want many applications over time, and all those will be organized under this umbrella. We will also decide that the restaurant will use the **Scrum** process as its development process.

First, we need to create the team project. For an on-premises installation, you can only do this from the Team Explorer within Visual Studio. For the TFS Service you can also do it from the **Welcome** page using the Web Access. We will show how to do it from Visual Studio, as follows:

1. Start Visual Studio.
2. Open Team Explorer (if you don't see it, go to the **View** menu and select **Team Explorer**):

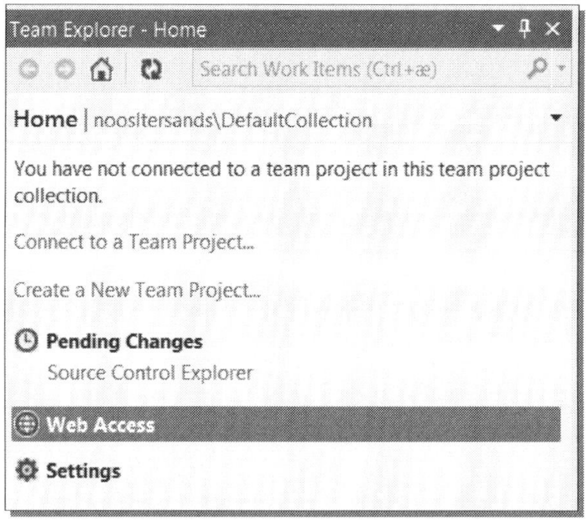

3. Select **Create a New Team Project...**.

4. Enter a name for the Team Project. The name can contain spaces, but since the name will also be part of the URL for the Team Project, and any space translates into `20%`, it is wise to skip the spaces in the Team Project name.

> Team project names cannot be changed after creation, so make sure that you pick a good name that will last.

5. Enter a suitable description and press **Next**.
6. You can now select between the available process templates. Accept the default **Scrum** template and press **Next**.
7. You can now select between creating a new empty **Source Control** folder, or branch from an existing one. We want the former, the default, so just press **Next** here too.
8. Select **Finish** on the last page, and the Team Project creation process will start. It usually takes around one or two minutes to create a team project.

Step 3 – Creating the team

We will now create the next level, which is the **Team**. In this case, we will equate a Team with an Application, since we will use the actual team (Terje, Jakob, and Meeta) for all the applications, but they will be managed separately.

1. Go to the Team's Web Access site, using the **Web Access** node of Visual Studio Team Explorer (from the **Home** tab):

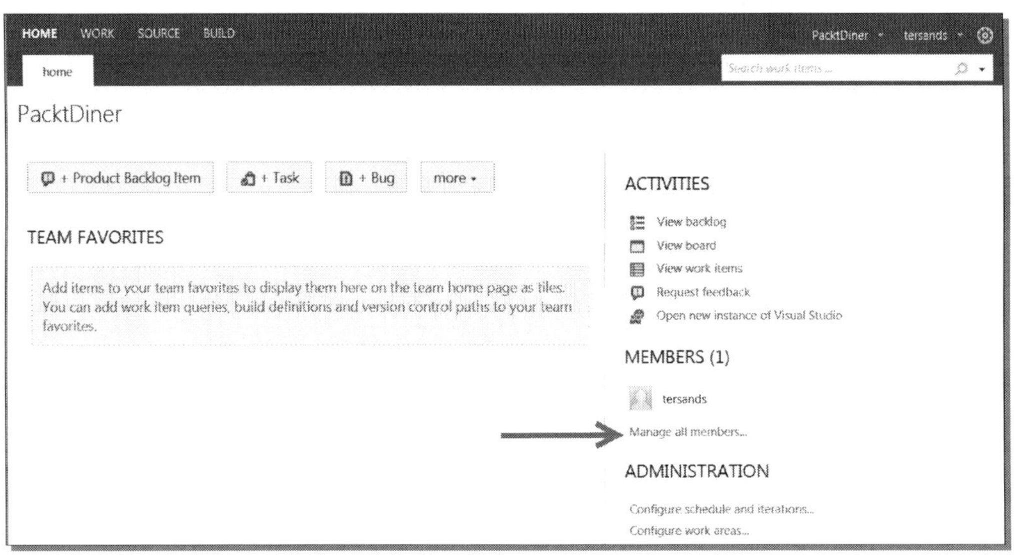

2. Select **Manage all members**.
3. Add the other Team members using the **Add** button.

Step 4 – Structuring areas for categorization and planning the release

Areas are used for categorization of work, and we will assign one area to the top level, which will match the application we are to make, and two sub-areas that will match the two functional levels Meeta wants us to develop, **Ordering** and **Payment**. She wants two releases of the product, and we plan to do these with two iterations/sprints each. Release planning is done using the **Iteration** feature.

1. Go to the Team's Web Access site, using the **Web Access** node of Visual Studio Team Explorer (from the **Home** tab):

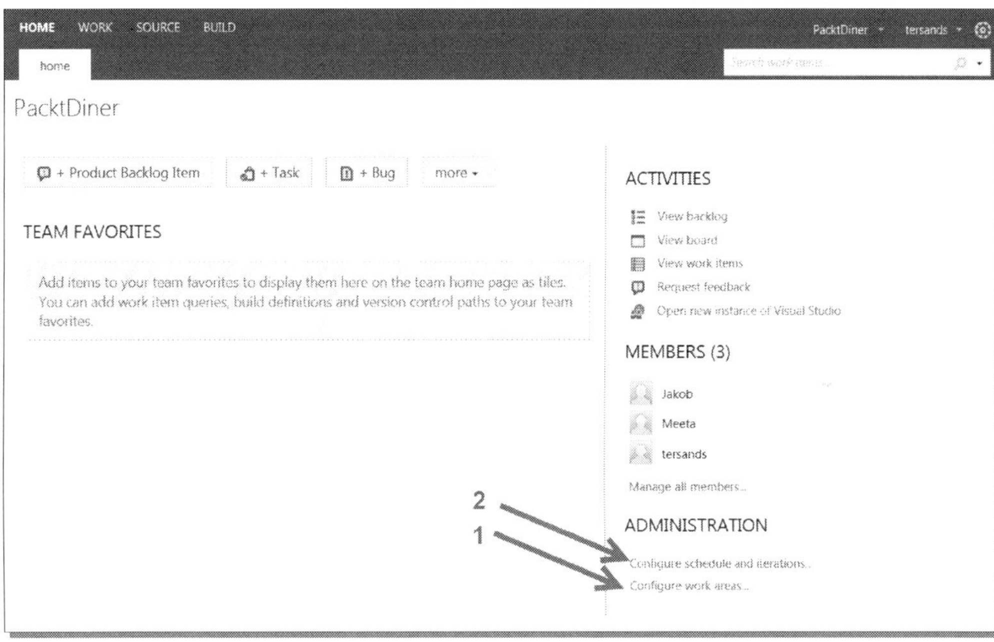

2. Select **1** (as marked in the preceding screenshot) for configuring the work areas.
3. Add a child named `WaiterApp`, which will be the name of our Application. Below this, add two child areas for Ordering and Payment; these are the two functional areas that we will develop.
4. Remove the checkbox in front of **PacktDiner** (ignore the warning that comes up)

5. Select the checkbox for the **WaiterApp**. Note that **default area** is also moved down to this area. It should now look similar to the following screenshot:

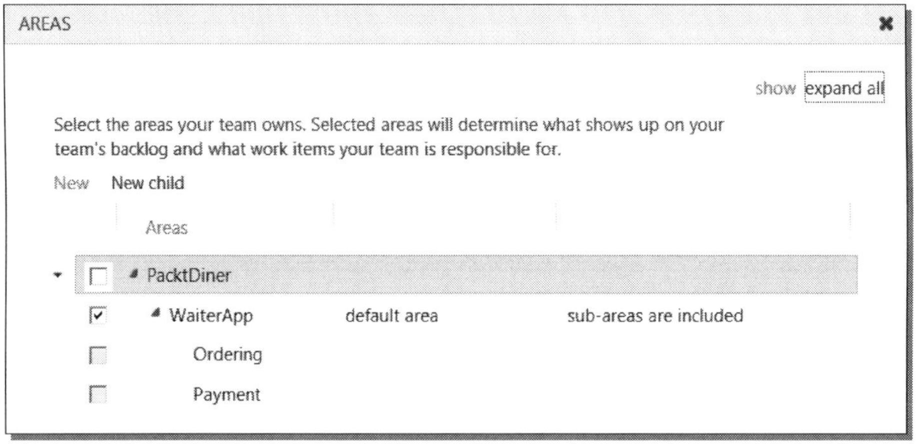

The areas are now set up as they need to be, and **WaiterApp** is associated with your team.

6. Now we will set up the release plan. Close the **Areas** dialog box, and click on **Configure schedule and iterations** (highlighted as **2** in the screenshot after step 1). You will see a default setup with releases and sprints.
7. We will prepare the plan for multiple applications, so add a new child below the root node, and name it `WaiterApp`.
8. Consider your company release strategy

   You have the following two choices:

   - Make all the developments follow the same schedule: In this case, use the Microsoft default. There is no requirement to include the application names below the `root` folder.
   - Let every development have its own schedule: In this case, follow our example and add the application names below the `root` folder.

9. Drag the **Release 1** and **Release 2** nodes under `WaiterApp`.
10. Decide upon the cadence for your sprints, and add dates to the two sprints in each release following that cadence. It is quite common to set sprint cadence to two or three weeks. You don't need to add dates to the release nodes.

    Dates are added to the sprint by selecting the sprint. A clickable **Set Dates** link appears, and from that you can set the start and end date of the sprint.

11. Delete the remaining sprints and releases by right-clicking on the nodes, and select **Delete**. You will be asked where to place any work items with that iteration path; just accept the default, since there are no work items yet.
12. Move the checked box to the **WaiterApp** iteration node.
13. Select the **WaiterApp** node, right-click and select **Set as team's backlog iteration**.
14. Select the checkboxes in front of the sprints.
15. Rename the four remaining sprints as shown in the following screenshot. Select each of them, right-click and open them to edit the names. We add a prefix to the sprint numbers to indicate the release numbers.

    It should now look similar to the following screenshot:

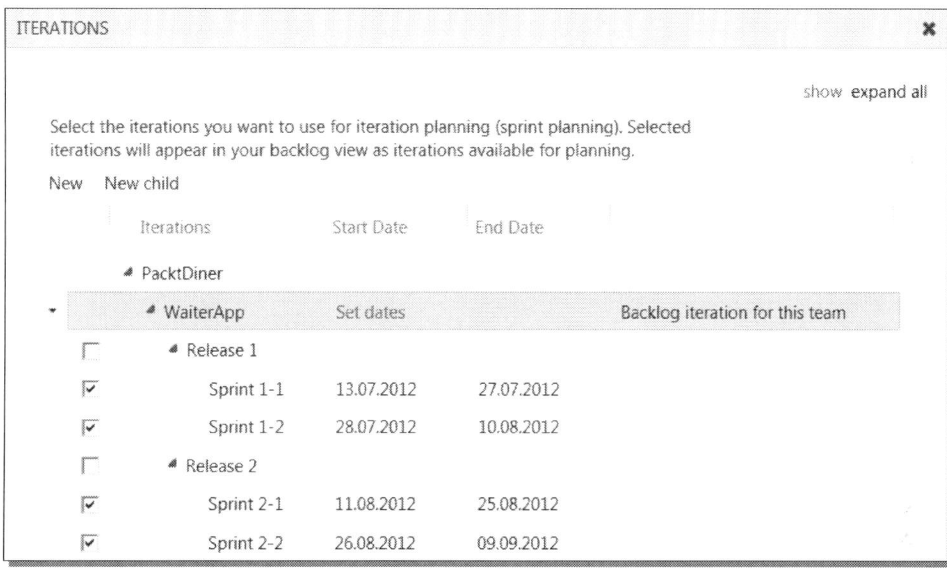

The functional categorization and release plan are now set up, and the team is associated with this project. All **Product Backlog Items** (**PBIs**) you want to include in the project should start out by having their iteration path set to **WaiterApp,** the backlog for this application.

Step 5 – Creating product backlog items

Meeta wants us to focus on two PBIs, namely **Place Order** and **Calculate Bill**. This will allow the waiter to take an order, using the Place Order user story, and to calculate the bill afterwards, using the Calculate Bill user story.

1. Go to the Team's Web Access site, using the **Web Access** node of Visual Studio Team Explorer (from the **Home** tab):

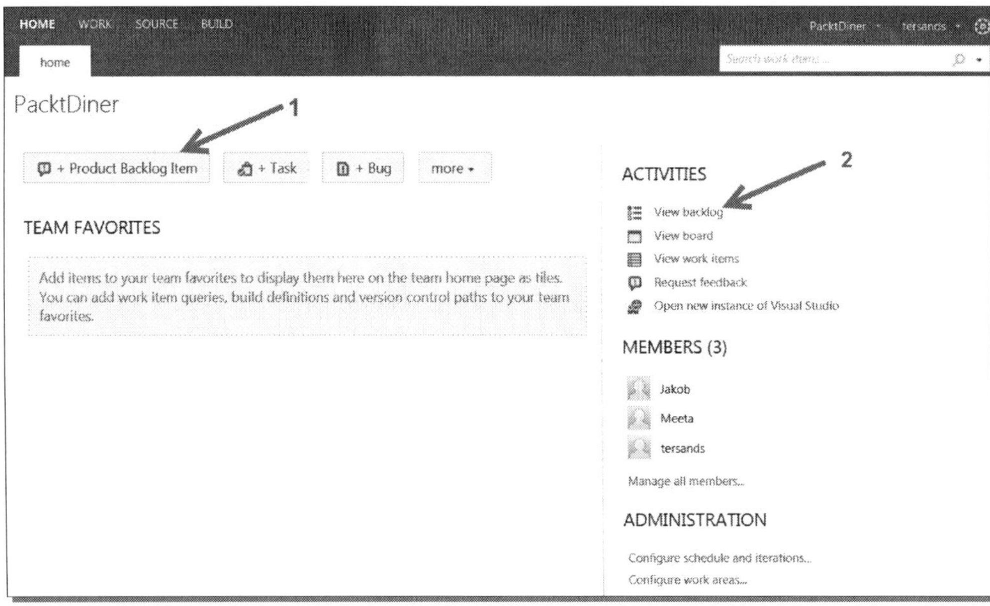

2. You can add the PBIs directly from this page by clicking on **Product Backlog Item** (marked as **1** in the preceding screenshot), which brings up a detailed work item form, or you can go to the **Backlog** view by clicking View Backlog (marked as **2** in the preceding screenshot), and add the items from there using a quick add function. For now, click on **1**, as we will add some more details than the quick add function allows.

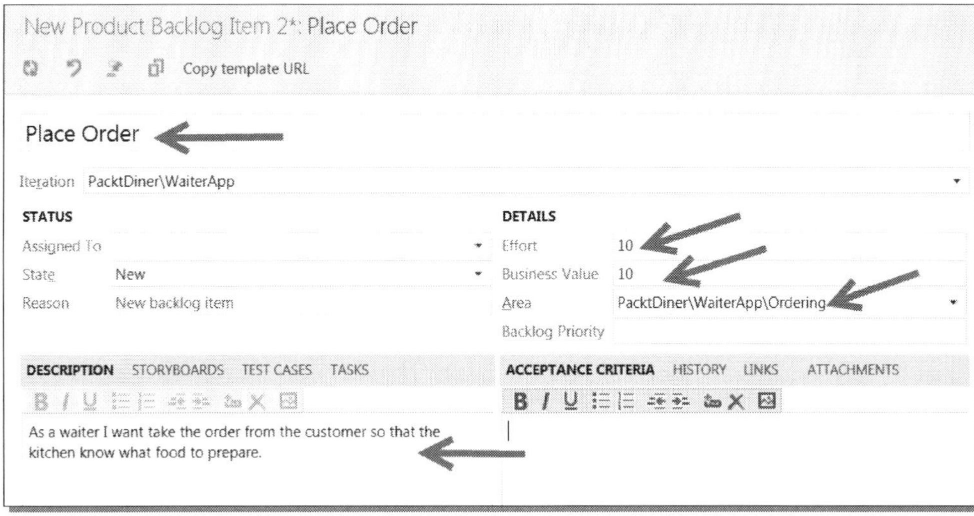

3. Change the information in the form as indicated in the preceding screenshot (indicated using the arrows).
4. Add another PBI named **Calculate Bill**, use the same values, but make the **Area** point to the **Payment** sub-area.

Step 6 – Assigning PBI to a sprint

We should now choose the first PBI for development in the first sprint. This is done in the **Product Backlog** view.

1. Select **View Backlog**.
2. Drag the **Place Order** user story over the **Sprint 1-1** node (arrow **1**):

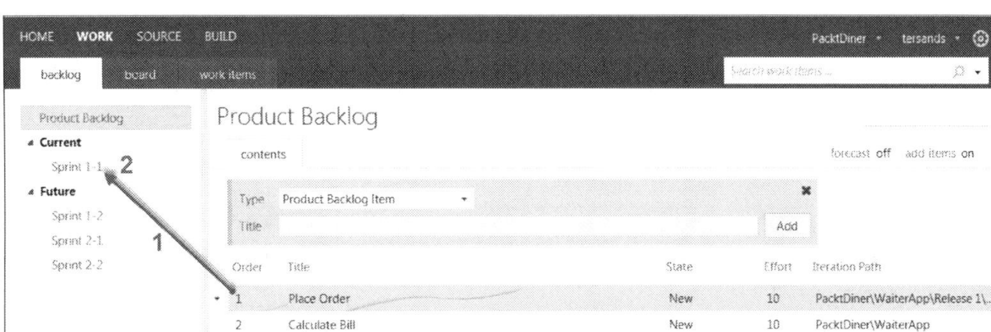

Step 7 – Creating subtasks

Each PBI should be split into tasks. The developer will work with tasks, and the sprint planning will be done by using tasks.

1. Select **Sprint 1-1**, (arrow **2** in preceding screenshot), to see the **Sprint 1-1** backlog.

   The **Place Order** user story will be shown in the list.

2. Press the **+** sign to add a task to the PBI, and set the title to **Implement UI**.

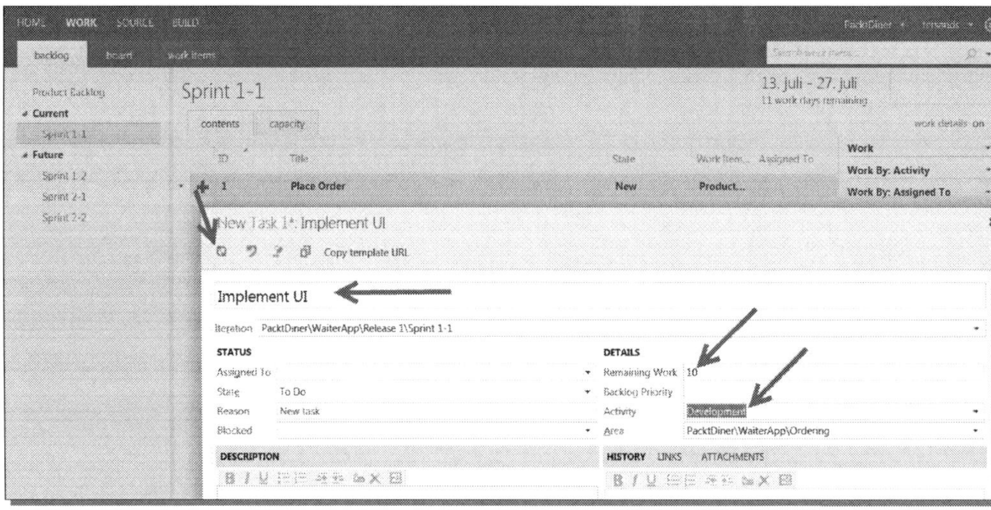

3. Add the 10 remaining hours, and set **Activity** to **Development**. Click on **Save and Close**.
4. Add two more tasks, **Implement Business Logic** and **Implement Storage Service**, in the same way.
5. Add a task named **Add test cases**, but set **Activity** to **Requirements**.

   The **Sprint Backlog** view should now look similar to the following screenshot:

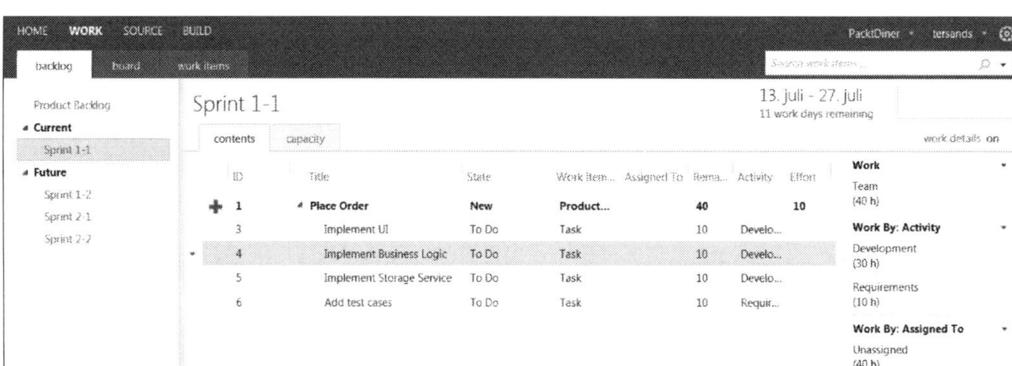

6. Add child work items "in context" of the PBI.

Note that the tasks we add here "inherit" some information, such as area and iteration paths, from their "parent". This is because we add the tasks "in context" of the parent PBI. Make a habit of always adding child tasks, test cases and bugs "in context" of the parent. You do that either from this backlog view or by opening the PBI and adding the items using the **New** button under one of the tabs—**Implementation**, **Test Cases**, or **All Links**.

Step 8 – Setting up the source control structure

To set up the source control structure, you use Visual Studio. We will add a structure that will allow further projects for other applications, and which will also allow for possible branching.

1. Go back to the **Team Explorer** node in Visual Studio, choose the **Home** node if not selected, and select the **Source Control Explorer** link button, found under the **Pending Changes** node (arrow **1** in following screenshot), to open up the **Source Control Explorer** window:

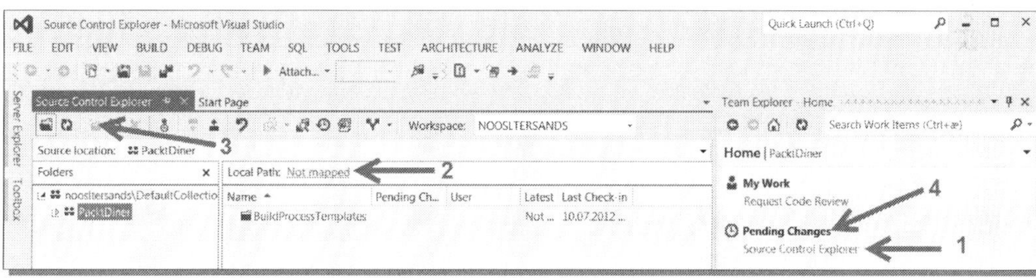

2. You need to map the source structure to a local disk. Press **Not mapped** (arrow **2** in preceding screenshot), and select a suitable location in the dialog box that appears (for example, `c:\PacktDiner`).

   Answer **No** to the question if you want to download all items.

3. The **Create Folder** button (arrow **3** in preceding screenshot) is now enabled. Create the folder structure as follows:

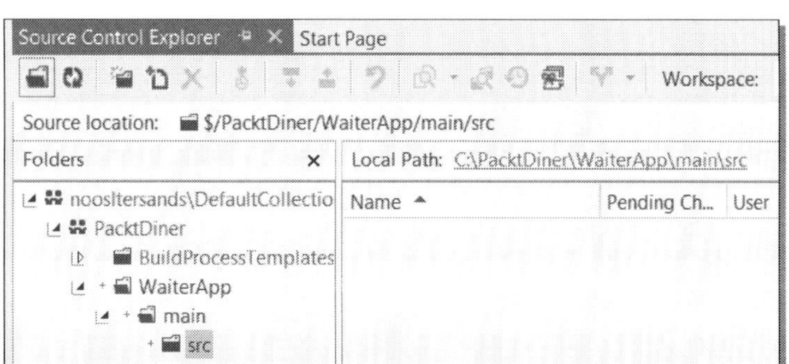

4. Click on the **Pending Changes** link in the **Team Explorer** node (arrow **2** in preceding screenshot).

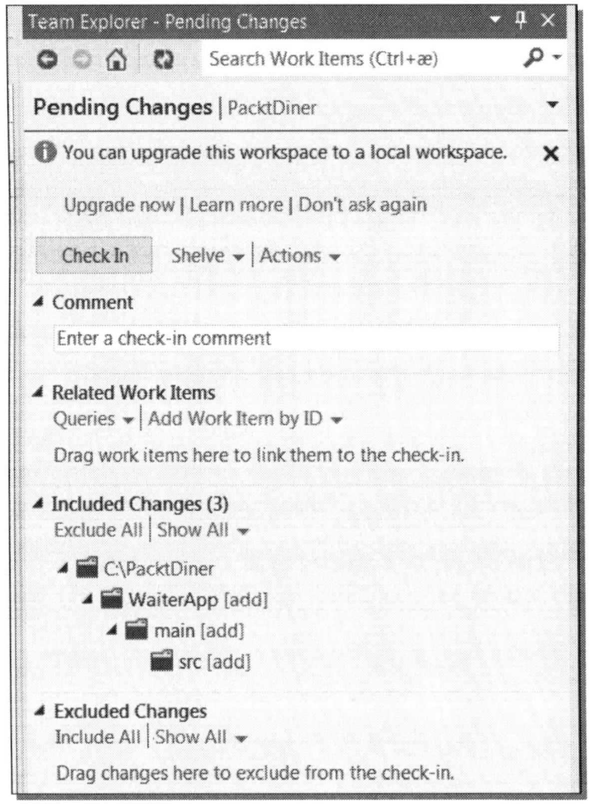

5. You will now be asked if you want to upgrade the workspace to a local workspace; answer by selecting **Upgrade now**.
6. Then enter some data for the **Comment** text area, such as `Folders added`, and click on the **Check In** button.

Step 9 – Adding solution to the source control

We will now add the code for the application to source control. We will use a readymade code snippet for this. In a normal situation, the developer would start out by creating a new solution, place the solution in the `src` folder, and add that to source control. Keep all code and libraries you need below the solution root folder (`src`). Avoid spreading them over multiple `root` folders. This will make the workspace setup much easier as you only need one mapping there, and there is less chance of mixing up the folder structure as it can be from a multiple root solution. If the workspace mapping gets too complex, it can also be hard to make it build correctly on the build server.

1. To save you the work of writing the code yourself, download the sample code from `http://www.packt.com/tfs2012starter/download/waiterapp.zip`.
2. Unzip the code and place it all under the `src` folder.
3. From the **Source Control Explorer** window, press the **Add files to source control** icon:

4. If you use a local workspace, TFS 2012 will pick up the added files and show them as **detected changes** in the **Pending Changes** view.
5. In the Team Explorer, under the **Home** tab, press **Pending Changes** and add a suitable comment, such as **Added waiter app solution**, and click on **Check In**.

Step 10 – Installing and configuring the build system

You should normally install the build system on a separate server. It may very well be a virtual server. If you're just playing around with the system or if there are very few developers, then you may install it to the same machine you have installed the TFS 2012 Server on.

1. Start the installation from the TFS install media, as mentioned in the *Installation* section.
2. When the **TFS Configuration** wizard appears, go to the **Build Configuration** tab and select **Configure Installed Features**.
3. Start the wizard and press **Next**.
4. On the **Project Collection** page, browse to the **DefaultCollection** URL (`http://TFSServer:8080/tfs`).
5. Add the recommend number of build agents, one per core of your server.
6. When selecting the build service account, select **Use a system account** and then choose **NT AUTHORITY\NETWORK SERVICE (default)**.
7. Run through the rest of the wizard.

Step 11 – Creating your first continuous integration build

You should always create a **Continuous Integration** (**CI**) build for your solutions. Make it a habit to have a consistent naming scheme for your builds. We will use the following pattern here: `ApplicationName.BuildType`, and in this case `WaiterApp.CI`.

1. Go to the **Team Explorer - Builds** window in Visual studio.

2. Select the **Builds** tab.

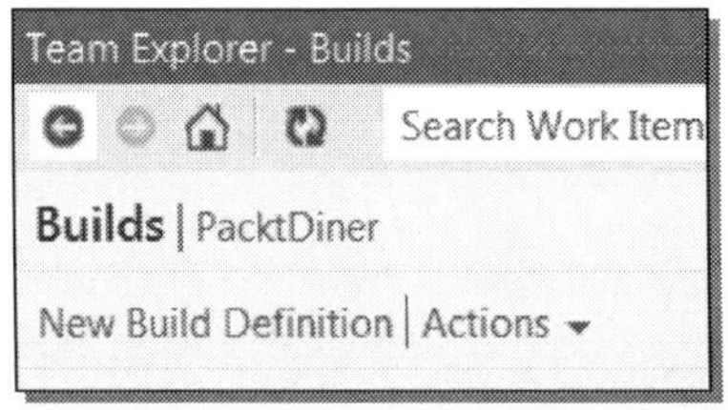

3. Select **New Build Definition,** and work through the tabs as follows:
   - **General**: Set the name to `WaiterApp.CI`
   - **Trigger**: Select **Continuous Integration**
   - **Workspace**: Click into the first row of the source folder column and change the folder here to `$/PacktDiner/WaiterApp/main/src`
   - **Build Defaults**: The controller you installed should already be visible and selected; if not, select it
4. Open **Explorer** on the build server. Create a folder named `Drops`.
5. Change the properties to make this folder a shared folder.
6. Check the permission to ensure that the account the build service is running under (often the local **Network Service** account is used) has complete control over this folder.
7. Add the name of the computer and folder to the **Staging location** field:

8. In the **Process** tab go to **Items to build,** and select **WaiterApp.sln**.
9. Save the build definition.
10. Right-click on the new build definition, and select **Queue a new build**.
11. After a little while, it is shown as a green build, which means that you have succeeded in setting up an integrated TFS 2012 environment.
12. Now, try to make some small changes in one of the files in the solution/project. Notice that the file is automatically checked out (red check mark). Right-click on the file, choose **Check In,** and you're taken to the **Pending Changes** tab. Add a comment and check in the file. Go to the **Builds** tab and notice that a new build has automatically started. After a while, it goes green (hopefully), indicating a successful build.

Step 12 – Naming

In the **Server URL** box, you should enter a nice name for your TFS service. Give this some consideration, as currently you can only have one site for an account. Also, you cannot rename this after it has been created. Use your own name or your company name here.

When you continue by clicking on **Create your account,** you're taken to the Live ID service. Log in with your Live ID:

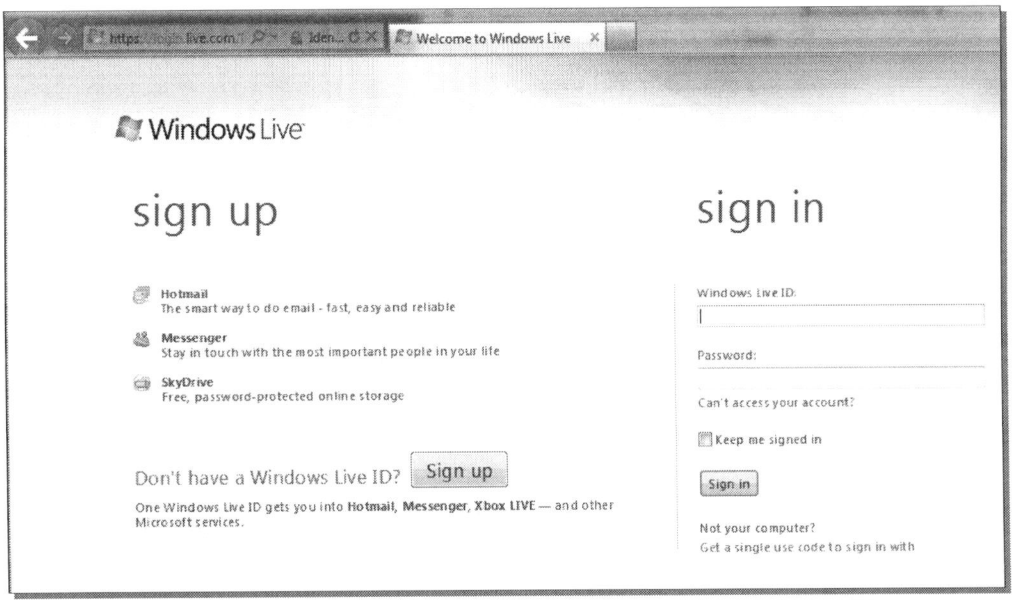

The integration with Windows Live ID is a big change compared to the on-premise version of TFS. Team Foundation Services doesn't currently support Active Directory integration.

Your account is now created and you're taken to the start page:

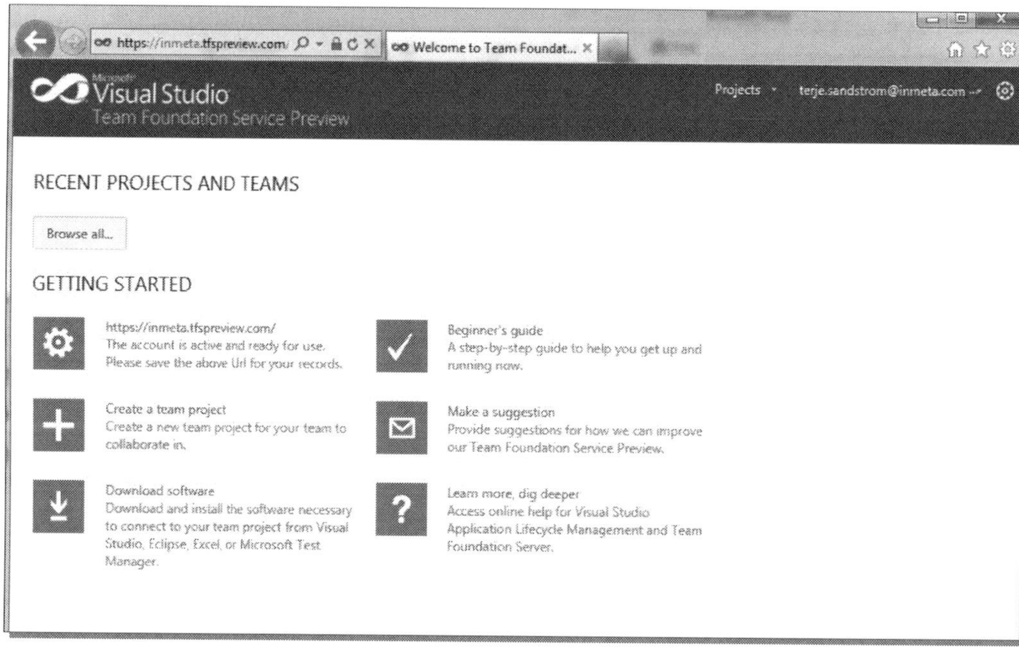

That's it; you now have access to TFS anywhere from a PC with an Internet connection! Note that this web access is the same as the one included included in the on-premise installs. In the **Top Features** section, you will learn how to get started using it.

What do I need on my client machine?

TFS 2012 can be accessed in many ways. The different roles can use different tools, as described in the introduction. If you are a developer, you can use any of the Visual Studio editions from VS 2005 and upwards, given that you have the appropriate updates for the earlier versions.

If you are a developer, you need a compatible Visual Studio version; one of these would suffice:

- **Visual Studio 2012** (Professional or above), install from: `http://www.microsoft.com/visualstudio/11/en-us/downloads`
- **Visual Studio 2008** or **2010** (Professional or above) with their respective forward-compatibility patches from `http://support.microsoft.com/kb/2673642` or `http://support.microsoft.com/kb/2662296`

The editions of Visual Studio 2012, which can access TFS 2012, are Professional, Premium, and Ultimate, or for testers the Microsoft Test Manager in the Test Professional SKU. Visual Studio Express can use TFS Express edition.

If you are developing code on non-Windows machines, for example using the Eclipse IDE, then you can use **Team Explorer Everywhere** (**TEE**) to access your TFS 2012 installation. Download TEE from `http://www.microsoft.com/en-us/download/details.aspx?id=29933`.

Users of Office Excel and Project 2007 and 2010 can access TFS 2012 by installing the Team Explorer, which also installs the required add-in components for Office.

When installing Visual Studio 2012, it will also install the required components for Office PowerPoint that can be used for storyboarding your applications.

Users who don't use any tools can still use the TFS 2012 Web Access with its new revamped Agile Workbench solution. For license details, see `http://www.microsoft.com/en-us/download/details.aspx?id=13350`.

Top features you'll want to know about

This section goes through the major important features of the TFS 2012, which you need to create a complete development workflow for the team.

1 – Team Explorer

The Team Explorer is the main point of access when working with TFS 2012. It ships as a part of Visual Studio 2012, but you can also install it separately. You access Team Explorer from **View | Team Explorer**.

Team Explorer consists of several "pages", where each page gives access to the main features of TFS. We will list them shortly here; the rest of this chapter expands on the top features.

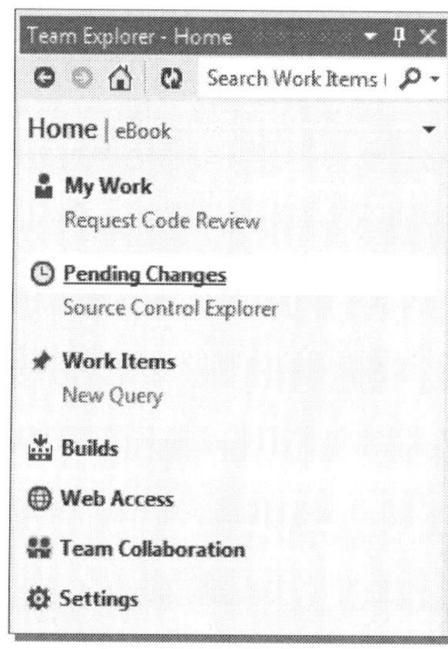

The **Home** page gives you links to the other pages, which are listed as follows:

- **My Work**: The developers will spend most of their time here. It displays only the work that is relevant for the developer, and provides an easy way to associate their changes with the correct work item.

  Also, this page lets developers suspend what they are currently doing to work on something else. When they are finished, they can resume the previous work, which includes modified source files, associated work items, windows that were open, and other IDE settings.

Last but not least, this page contains an integrated workflow for doing code reviews. This page is available in **Premium** and **Ultimate** editions. For more information on how to do code reviews in Visual Studio 2012, see `http://msdn.microsoft.com/en-us/library/hh474795.aspx`.

Note that the **My Work** page is only available in the Visual Studio Premium Edition and above.

- **Pending Changes**: This page shows all the changes that are done locally and haven't yet been checked in. The changes can be associated to work items, and can also be shelved in order to start working on something else, for example.
- **Work Items**: This page shows all work item queries in the current team project, and lets users create new queries that can be shared with the rest of the team.
- **Builds**: This page gives access to all build definitions in the team project. You can also manage the build resources, for example the build controllers and build agents that will execute your builds.
- **Web Access**: This is just a link to the web access portal for the current team project.
- **Team Collaboration**: If you have installed the Team Foundation Server Power Tools, then Team Explorer will integrate with Microsoft Lync and MSN Messenger in order to promote communication within the team. This hub shows the status for each team member (if they are running Microsoft Lync or MSN Messenger) and lets you see TFS-related information about them, such as their check-in history.
- **Settings**: This page shows links to all the administration tasks that can be done, both for the current team project and the team project collection. Most of these links will redirect the user to the web access to complete the task, but some are available inside the Team Explorer.

2 – Version control

Version control is the heart of TFS 2012. You use version control to store your source code and any other artifacts that are a part of the development of your products. In this section, you will learn about the core features and concepts of TFS 2012 version control.

Source control explorer

The **Source Control Explorer** window (available from the **Home** page in the Team Explorer) shows a full source control repository for the team project collection. Basically, it works in a manner similar to Windows Explorer and lets you browse, search, and perform actions on files and folders.

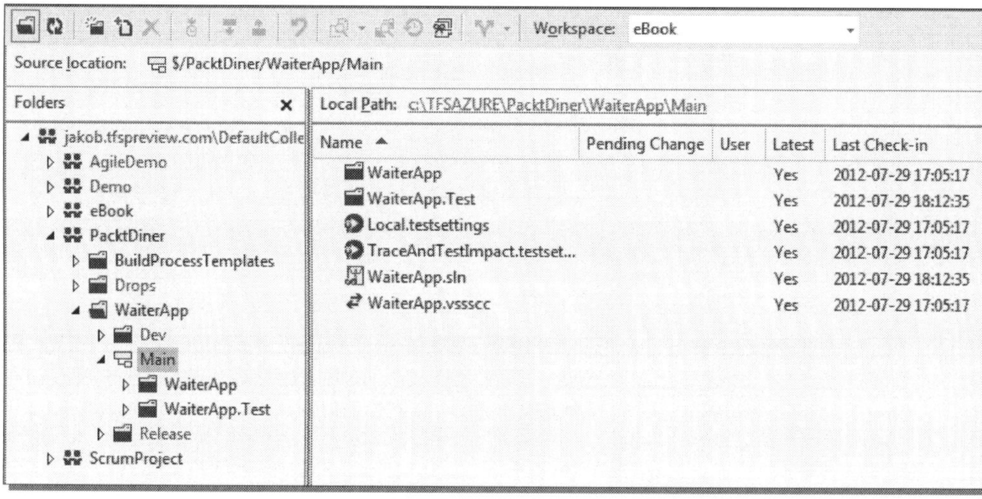

Workspaces

The **workspace** is a mapping between the TFS source control repository and your local development machine. You must create at least one workspace before you can download and modify anything in the source control. There are two types of workspace, namely **Server workspaces** and **Local workspaces**.

A local workspace is new to TFS 2012 and allows for local work in offline scenarios. You can check out, add, and remove files when offline. It synchronizes with the server when you're online again. The server workspace, on the contrary, keeps all the information about your workspace on the server.

> You should, in most cases, use local workspaces. It is faster and has much better offline support than server workspaces. Consider using server workspaces only for very large codebases.

Changesets

Every time you check in one or more modified source files, TFS bundles these files together into a changeset. A **changeset** contains the modified source files, and the following information:

- A Changeset ID that is unique across a Team Project Collection
- A comment written by the person who performed the check-in
- The date and time of the check-in
- One or more associated work items
- Check-in notes, which can be used for code reviews and auditing
- Violations of check-in policies

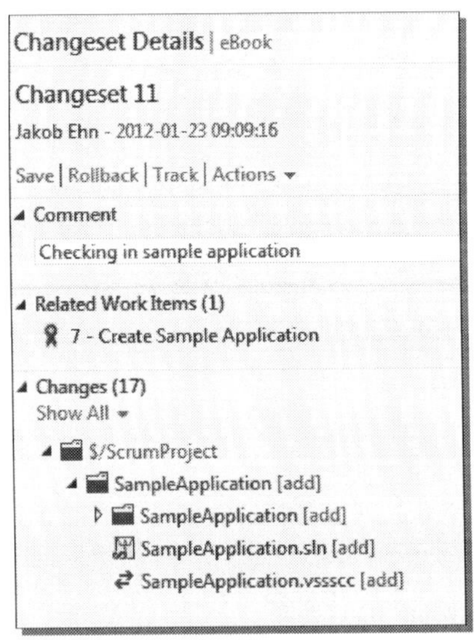

A changeset is atomic, meaning that it will either be fully committed to TFS or, in case of any error, not committed at all.

Pending changes

All the changes that are you are currently working on are automatically added to the set of pending changes. Every type of change is a pending change, including edits, moves, branches, and deletes. It is not until you check in your pending changes that these are committed to the TFS source control repository as a changeset.

The **Pending Changes** tab will show the files as included if they match the Team Explorer rules for files to include by default. Normally, these files are a part of the current solution. The remaining modified files in your workspace will be shown under excluded. You can move files between included and excluded by dragging them between their headings:

Get Latest/Get Specific

When you want to download the latest changes that have been checked in, you need to right-click and select **Get Latest Version** in the source control explorer.

Sometimes, you will need to get another specific version of a file or project. This is done by using the **Get Specific Version** command, located under the **Advanced** sub-menu in the source control.

History

TFS keeps a track of all changes made to the items in the source control and users who performed the change. Often, you will want to view the history of a file or a complete folder, which can be done right in the source control explorer:

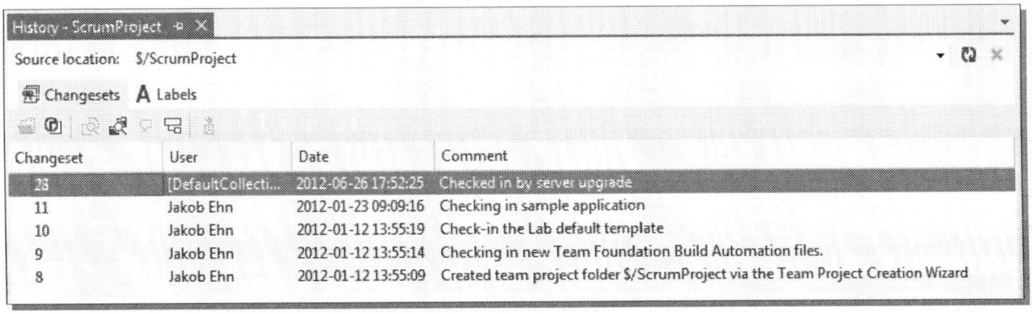

You can view details of each changeset within the history list, and you can also compare the differences for a file or folder between any given versions:

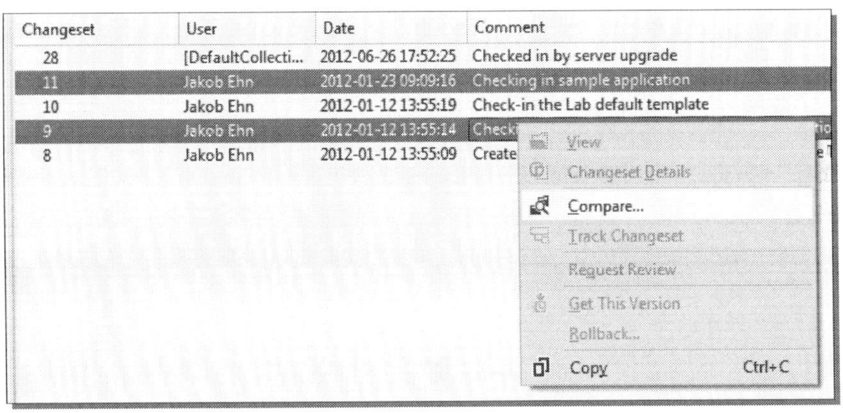

Annotate

When looking at the source code, you will often find yourself wondering who wrote that code and why. You can answer this question by using the **Annotate** function. It will show which user had last modified any particular line of code, with a link to the corresponding changeset.

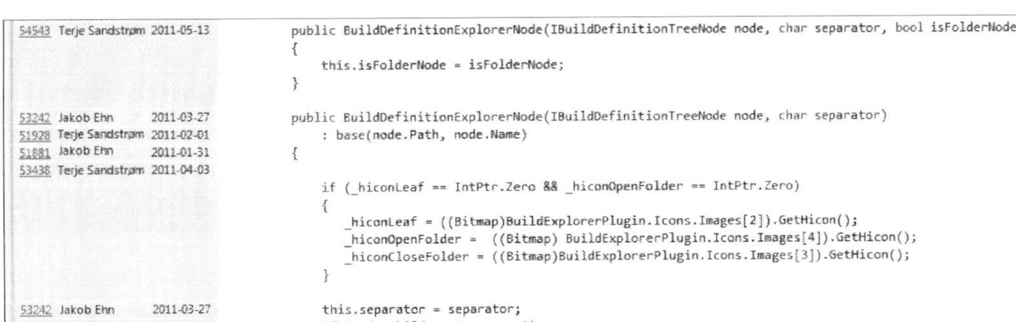

When clicking on the link in the left bar, you will get the full changeset details, including comments and work items that should answer why the change was made.

Shelving

Sometimes, you may work on a new feature that is partly done and suddenly get interrupted by something else. At such times, you may not want to keep your changes lying around on your local machine, but commit them back into the main repository. These changes might not even compile. This is one occasion where shelvesets are very useful. A **shelveset** is basically a changeset that is not checked into the main repository. You can gain several benefits by shelving your changes, a few of which are listed as follows:

- The changes are stored and backed up together with the rest of the repository
- You can "unshelve" the changes onto another machine
- Other team members can unshelve your changes onto their machine, for reviewing your code or helping you out with something

Use private builds to build a shelveset

Shelving will not trigger any automatic builds. You can still build a shelveset by choosing **Latest sources with shelveset** in the **Queue Build** dialog box. This is called a **private build**.

Branching and merging

When setting up the source code structure for a new project, you should always prepare for branching. To support branching, you need to make sure that the project is contained within a top-level node that indicates which branch it belongs to. The following screenshot is an example:

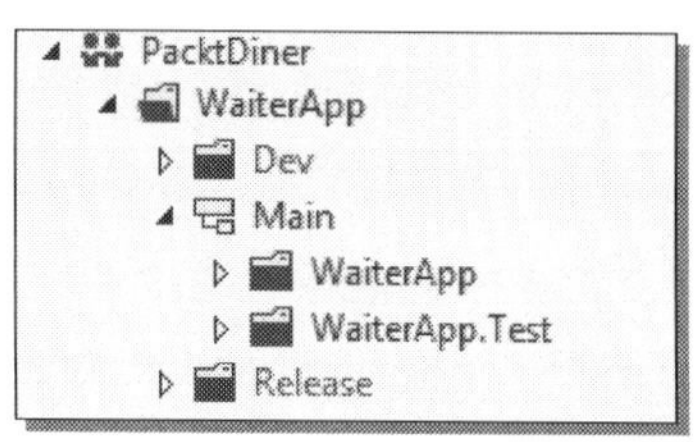

We have created a **Main** branch, where the source will be added in the beginning of the project. Later on, you can branch from the **Main** folder. Here we have created a **Dev** folder that will contain the development branches and a **Release** folder, which will contain the released branches. This will make sure that **Main** is the parent of all other branches, and any changes that are done must flow through the **Main** branch.

To create a new branch, select a folder in the source control explorer, right-click and select **Branching and Merging | Branch**.

In this example, we create a branch from the **Main** folder (source) and name the **Target** (child) branch **Release\1.0**.

A common scenario is that a bug may occur in production that needs to be fixed as soon as possible. We can fix the bug in the **Release** branch and build a new version of the product. Later, we need to merge the bug fix back to **Main**. Do this by selecting the **Release/1.0** branch in source control, and select **Branching and Merging | Merge**.

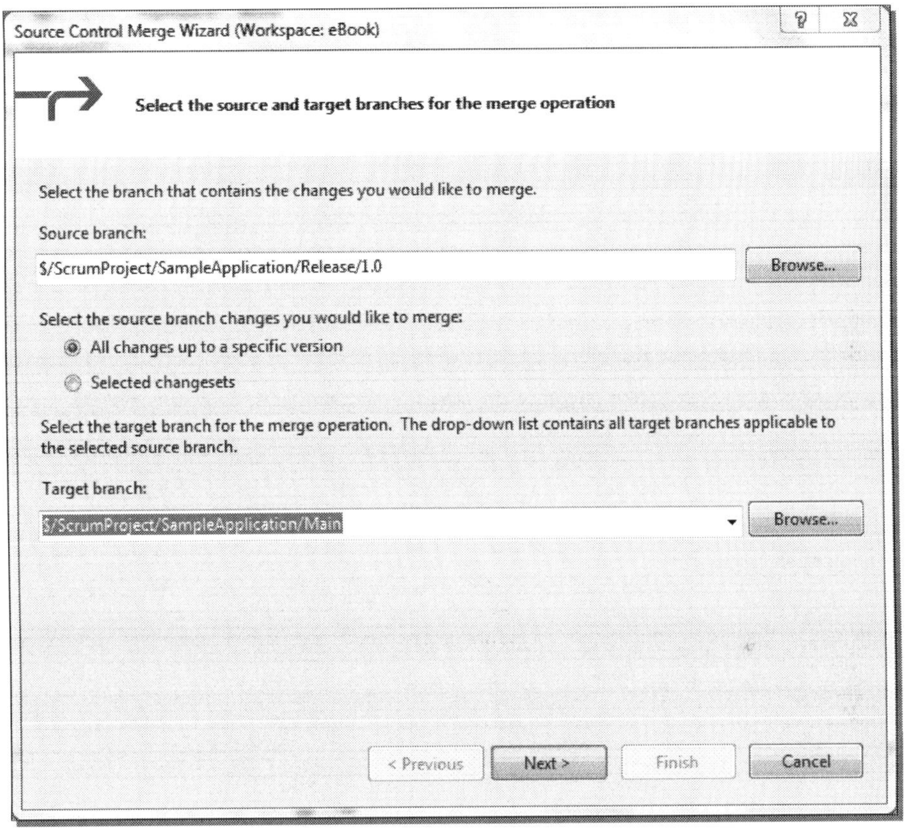

In the preceding dialog box, we can select the source and the target branches (we can only select the branches that are either a child or a parent of the source branch). We can also select to merge all the changes up to a specific version (often the latest version), or select specific changesets (often called a **Cherry Pick Merge**).

Branch hierarchies can grow complex over time, making it hard to visualize how they are connected to each other. To view the branch hierarchy, select **Branching and Merging | View Hierarchy**.

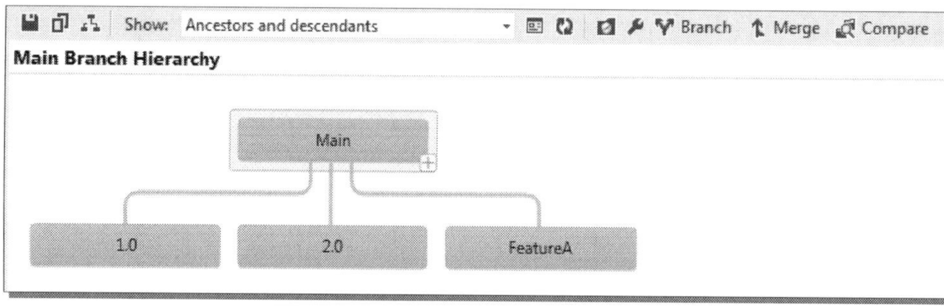

In the preceding screenshot, you can see a branch hierarchy where the **Main** branch has three child branches—one development branch (**FeatureA**) and two release branches (**1.0** and **2.0**).

> **Give branches meaningful names**
>
> When visualizing branches, only the branch name is visible so give them meaningful names. For example, `ProjectName_1.0` instead of just `1.0`, but keep in mind the total path length limits (260 chars on file, and 399 chars in source control after TFS 2012 Update 1).

Tracking across branches

A bug is initially fixed in one of the branches. Use the **Track Changeset/Work Item** feature in TFS to see where the work item or changerset was initially resolved and to which branches the change have been merged.

In the following example, we have a bug (ID 27) that was initially fixed in the **Release 1.0** branch:

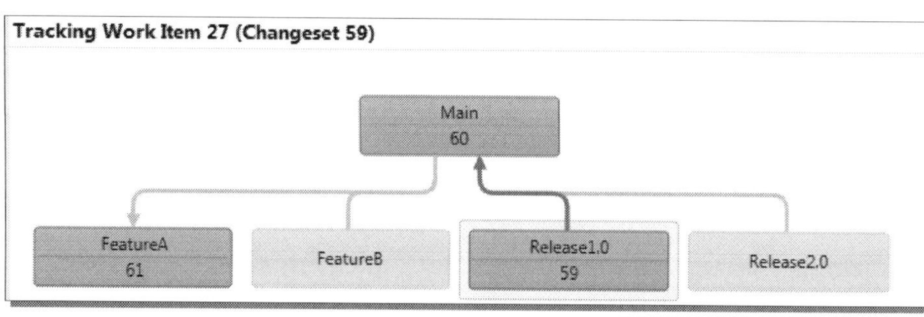

As indicated by the colors, the bug fix was merged to **Main** (Changeset 60) and then it was merged to the **FeatureA** development branch (Changeset 61). However, it has NOT been merged to the **FeatureB** or the **Release 2.0** branch.There is also a **Timeline Tracking** view that shows the same information in time sequence, which can be very useful.

> **Merge changes by drag-and-drop between the branches**
> In both these views, we can merge the changes by dragging the boxes between the branches. The drag/drop operation will open the **Merge** dialog box.

The Visual Studio ALM Rangers have published a branching guidance, containing industry best practices; see `http://vsarbranchingguide.codeplex.com/`.

3 – Work items

You must use **work items** when you need to track work in TFS. Work items exist in different types, for tracking a specific type of work that needs to be done.

The set of work item types you have available is determined by the process template you selected while creating the Team project. TFS comes with different process templates. These can be thought of as blueprints for new team projects, and may contain default information for work item types, default permissions, and build templates.

One of the most popular process templates is the Microsoft Visual Studio Scrum 2.0 process template , which contains the following main work item types:

- **Product Backlog Item**: These work items are the work that a product owner wants to be implemented and that can be prioritized against other items on the backlog.
- **Task**: PBIs are broken down into smaller Task work items. Each Task work item can then be assigned to a developer for implementation.
- **Bug**: These work items represent a bug that has occurred either in production or during internal testing. Bugs are normally prioritized against other PBIs on the backlog
- **Impediment**: An impediment in scrum is something that stops the team from finishing their sprint goal.

Here is an example of a work item of the PBI type:

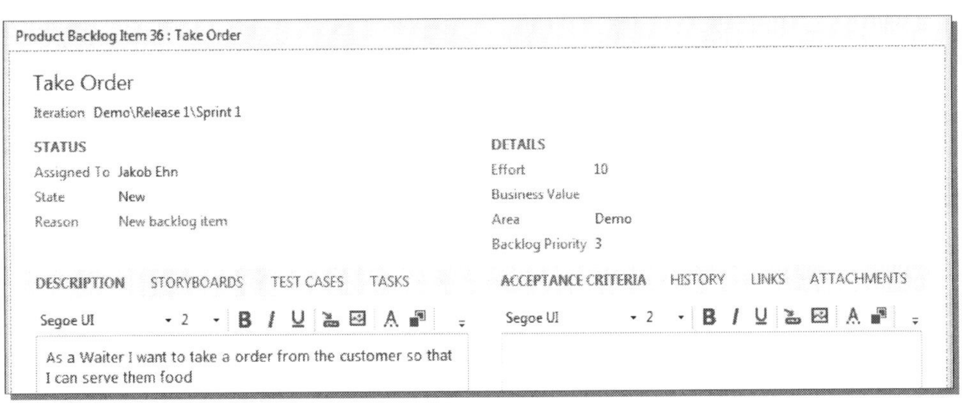

In this work item type, there are a total of eight different tabs that contain information. TFS 2012 Power Tools includes a tool that lets you customize process templates and work item types using a GUI. After the power tools have been installed, you can access the features from **Tools | Process Editor**.

> When customizing work item types, start from one of the existing work item types and make your modifications to it.
>
> Also, it's best practice to keep your work items under the source control. Create a separate team project to keep all your TFS-related artifacts.

For more information on Work Item Type customization, see `http://msdn.microsoft.com/en-us/library/ms195025(v=vs.90).aspx`.

Creating work items

There are several tools at your disposal when it comes to creating (and viewing) work items in TFS. When creating one or a few work items, you will normally use either Team Explorer or TFS Web Access.

The following screenshot shows how it looks in the Team Explorer. From the **Work Items** page, you can create new top-level work items from the menu:

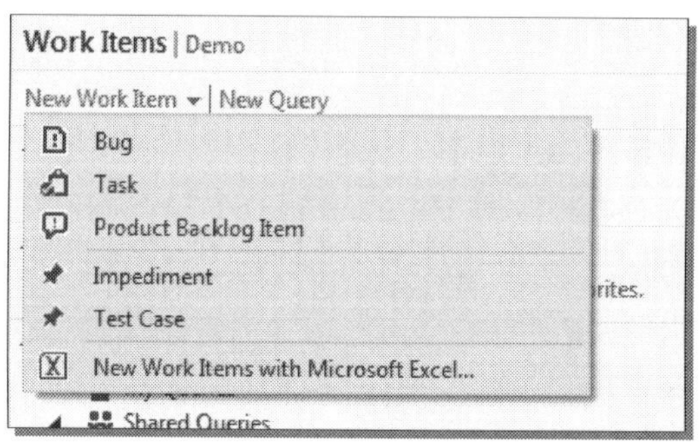

Subsequent child work items are created inside the parent work item form. Every work item can be linked to many other artifacts in TFS, such as other work items, source control changesets, and external URLs. This is a core feature that enables full traceability in your project between requirements, design, implementation, testing, and deployment.

You create links to other items of a variety of types by using the **Links** tab, and pressing either **New** or **Link to**.

The most common link type is **Parent/Child**. This is most commonly used to break down work into smaller tasks. Since this is so common, there is a separate tab called **Tasks** in the **Product Backlog Item** work item type. This lets you create subtasks for your PBI that are automatically linked as children.

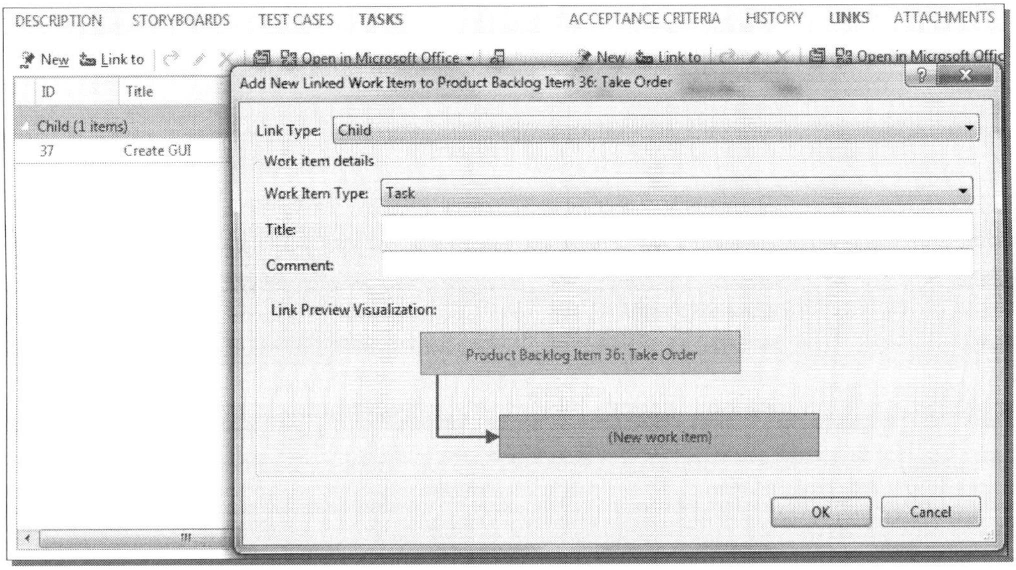

Another important tab is the **Test Cases** tab. This lets you create test cases (which are a work item type as well) for your requirements. You will learn more about this later in this section.

> **Prefer to use the specialized tabs**
>
> You should prefer to use the specialized tabs of the PBI for implementation and test cases. Any work item created using these tabs will also inherit other relevant information, such as the Area Path and the Iteration Path.

Querying work items

You can find work items in three ways:

- **Work item ID**: Select **Team | Go To Work Item** and then enter the ID of the work item that you want to find
- **Searching the work items box in team explorer**: This lets you search for any string value in all the work items in the current team project.
- **Refining your search by adding search filters**: You can filter by **Assigned To, Created By, State and Work Item Type**. Each filter type can be expressed by a compact syntax, such as `C:"@Me"`, which will only return work items that were created by the current user.
- **Work item queries**: This is the most powerful way to access a list of work items. Since they can be saved and accessed by all team members, they are the main way to organize your project management.

A query can have several AND and OR clauses that filter the result; clauses can be grouped, and each query can be configured to return a specific set of columns and sort the order.

> **Prefer fewer queries**
>
> Avoid having too many queries, as they tend not to be used. Prefer a few good queries that are well used. Note that you can add your own queries to **My own queries**. This will avoid the team queries from getting clutter up.

Here is an example of a work item query that returns all the tasks in **Sprint 1** that are blocked:

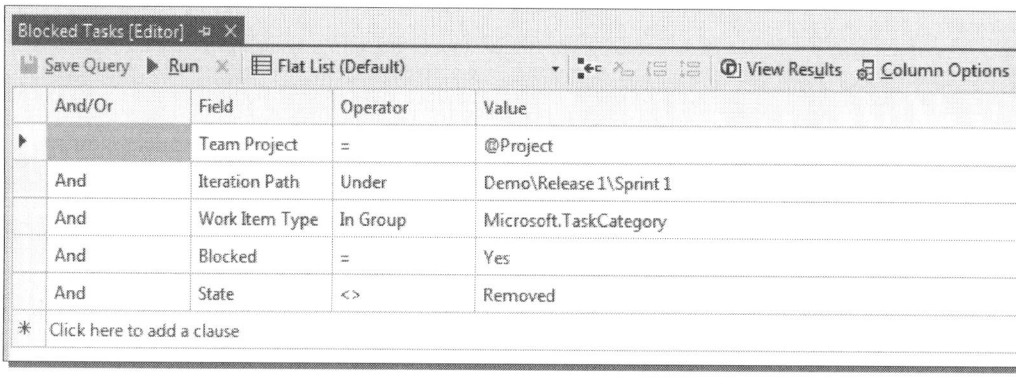

This query contains five different clauses, each of which filters in a different field. Clauses can be grouped by marking them and selecting **Group**.

Work item queries exist in three different flavors:

- **Flat list**: This returns a list of work items that matches the filters. No linked work items are returned.
- **Work items and direct links**: This returns the work items and any work items that are directly linked. Filters can be set for both the root and the link levels.
- **Tree of work items**: This returns a hierarchical set of work items; meaning all matching work items and their children recursively.

Work item queries are organized per team project in a hierarchical fashion, using folders to separate groups of queries:

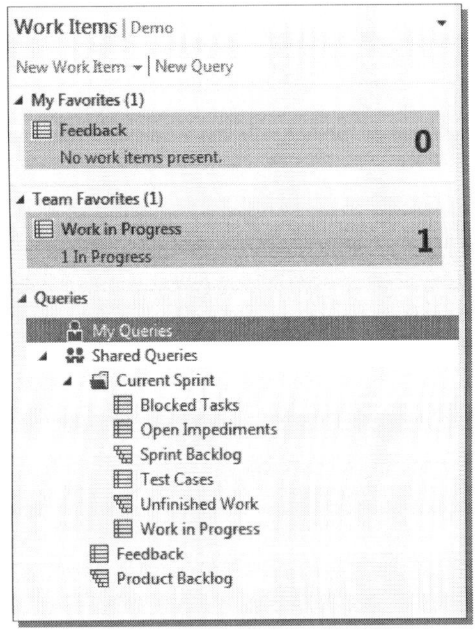

Current Sprint is a folder, which contains all the queries that apply to the current sprint. Note that this is only a convention, and there is no semantic relationship between the folder and the queries it contains. Also note that you can add work item queries to either **My Favorites** or **Team Favorites,** which also shows the total number of work items that those queries returned the last time they were executed.

> **Organize folders per team**
>
> If you use multiple applications per-team project, then you should mimic the same organization in the work item queries. Make one folder per application (or per "team", since team = application). Under each such folder, arrange the rest of the hierarchy in the same fashion.

Using Microsoft Excel for batch updating

Updating a few work items using either Team Explorer or the Web Access works fine, but often you will need to update many work items at the same time. In this scenario, you can use Microsoft Excel to batch update work items at the same time.

When using work item queries, you can right-click on them and select **Open in Microsoft Excel,** which will show the results of the query inside it. This works for all types of Work Item Queries; for example, flat lists, with direct links, and tree of work items.

Here is how the PBI query looks in Microsoft Excel:

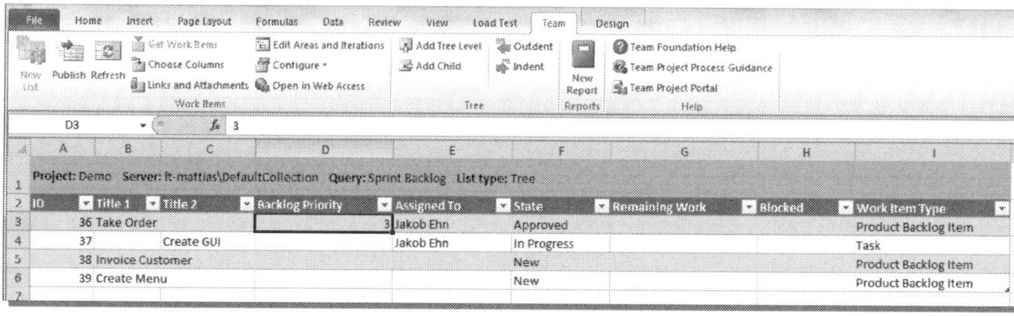

When you install TFS 2012 Team Explorer (or Visual Studio 2012) on a computer that has Microsoft Excel installed, the **Team** ribbon is created. This is what makes the Excel TFS aware and lets you work efficiently with work items.

Since Excel cannot show a hierarchical date, it flattens the result by adding extra columns for each level.

To create a new child task for the **Take Order** PBI, select the row containing the **Take Order** work item and then press the **Add Child** button in the **Team** ribbon:

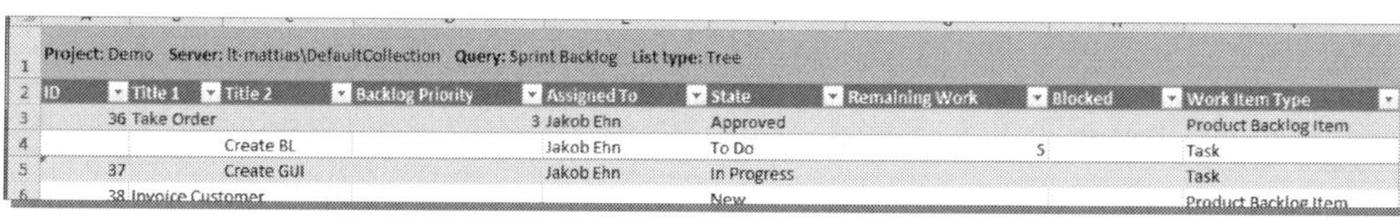

When the work item is saved, it will be given an ID (shown in the **ID** column). Press the **Publish** button to save.

> **Work item validation**
>
> All work items are validated as part of the publish operation. Any information outside the allowed values for a work item will not be transferred, and you will be informed about the columns that contain errors.

The My Works hub

The **My Work** hub contains all the artifacts that you are involved with during your work, across types. Work items can be activated (move to **In Progress**) directly in the hub, and you will also see all the code review feedback you're involved in.

The **Implement UI** task is available here. You can drag it directly to **In Progress Work Items & Changes,** to tell that you're now working on this item:

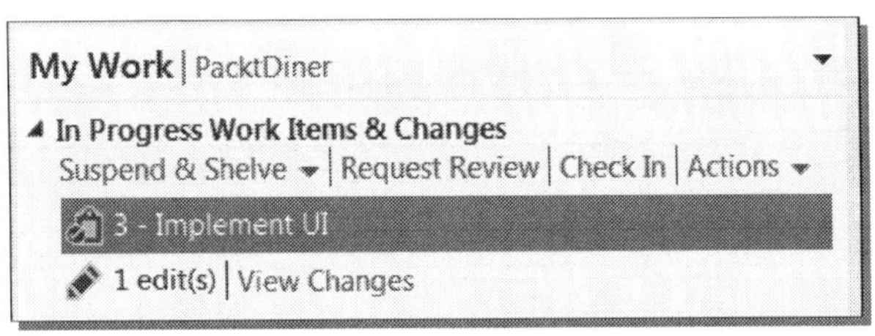

When you do this, it will automatically change the state to **Active** and become associated with the current pending changes.

4 – The Agile planning tools

In TFS 2012, the TFS Web Access was rewritten in order to fully embrace the concept of Agile planning. This includes concepts such as Product Backlogs, Sprint Backlogs, Tasks, and Kanban boards, and is a common practice among teams who practice Agile methodologies.

In the *Quick Start* section, we covered iteration planning and setting up a product backlog. We will now expand on this with the remaining features.

Product and sprint backlogs

A **product backlog** is central in Agile planning; this should contain everything that needs to be done for the corresponding product. Items in the product backlog are prioritized by their order on the backlog in a top to down manner.

To prioritize, you drag-and-drop the items:

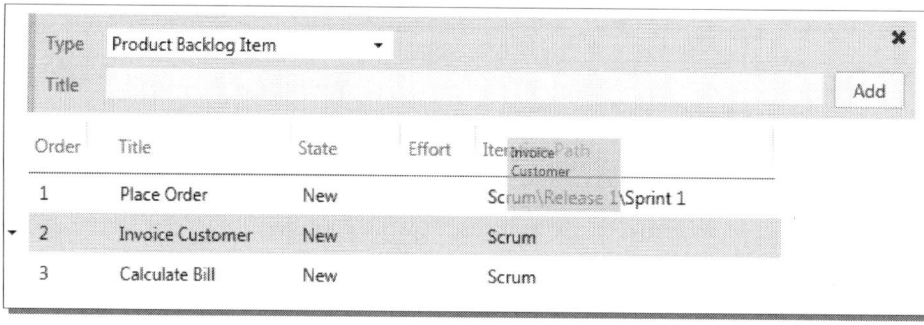

To assign items to sprints, you select the item on the backlog and drag it to the sprint on the left of the screen. You will see the **Iteration Path** field update automatically when you do this.

To view the sprint backlog, click on the **sprint** link on the left side of the screen. This will show all the backlog items that are assigned to the selected sprints and their tasks:

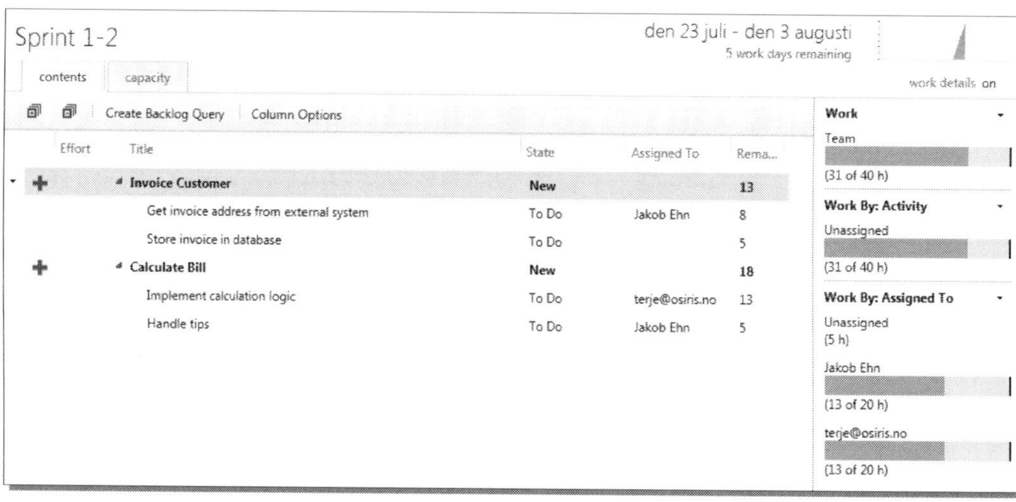

You can add new subtasks to the backlog items by clicking on the large plus icon (+) to the very left.

To the right, you can see the current capacity information for the current sprint. It shows how much of the total work is assigned to the team in this sprint (40 hours in this case) and how much of that work is allocated to each person and to the team in total (31 hours). In this case, the sprint looks OK; we haven't over allocated the team. If we add too much work, the fields will be marked with red color.

To be able to show this information, you need to define the capacity of each team member. This is done for each sprint and is done by clicking on the **capacity** tab:

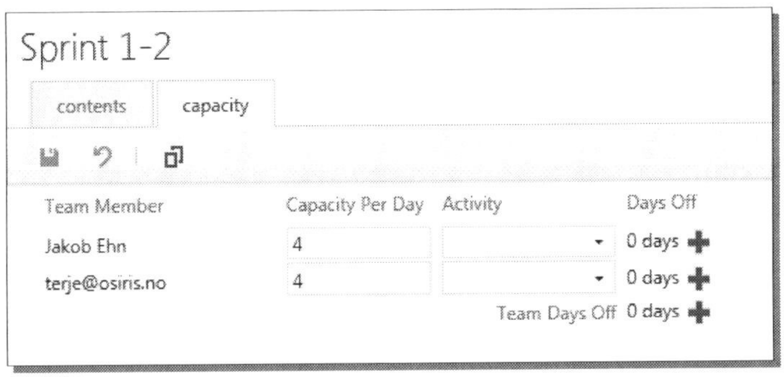

You set the capacity to how many hours per day each member can contribute (also restricting it to a certain activity), and to how many days during the sprint they will not be able to commit.

Using the Task and Kanban boards

Development starts when the sprint is fully planned. During the course of the sprint, you normally have a daily stand-up meeting, where each team member briefly describes what they have been doing, what they will do today, and if they have any impediments. It is also a good moment to go through the remaining work for each task that is assigned to them. When doing this, you use the **board** task in the TFS Web Access:

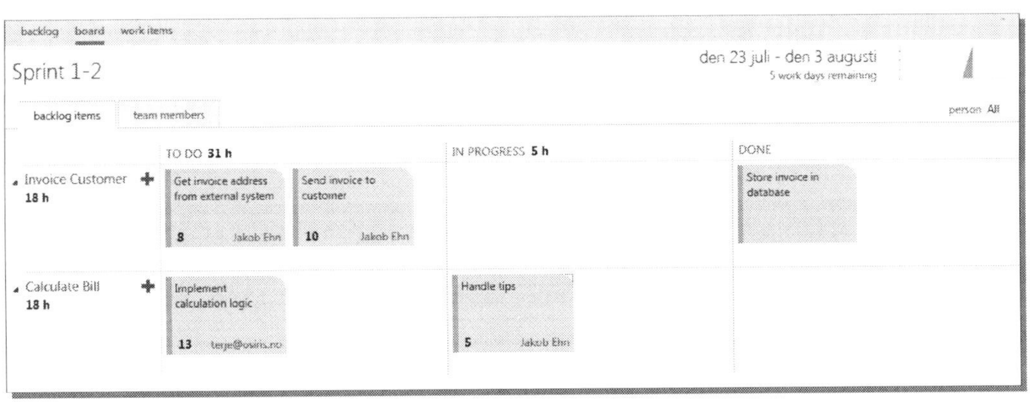

The **board** task shows all the backlog items to the left, with the total numbers of hours of remaining work below. All the implementation tasks are shown to the right in the corresponding state column.

In the upper-right corner, a small burn-down graph is shown; you can expand it by clicking on it. This is always up-to-date. Every time you change the remaining work or add a new task, the burn-down graph will reflect it immediately.

To change the state of a task, just drag it from the left to the right. Under the hood, TFS will update the necessary fields. You can easily assign a work item to another team member by clicking on the name in the task. You can also change the remaining work by clicking on the number in the lower-left of the task:

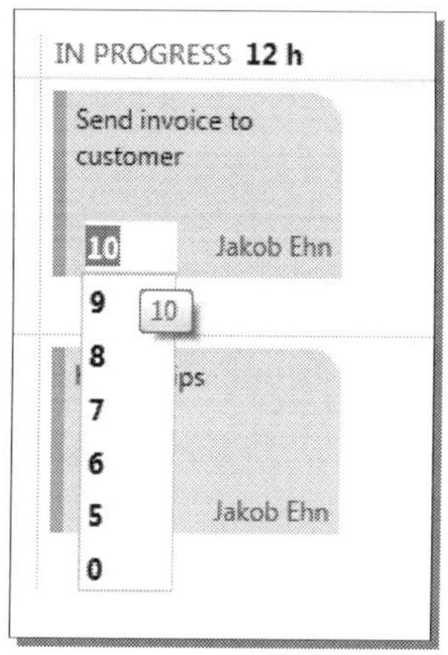

When you drag a task from **IN PROGRESS** to **CLOSED, Remaining Work** will automatically be cleared.

> **Prefer to create small tasks**
>
> Keep your tasks small. If they get too large, it will be too difficult to estimate the remaining, or even knowing if you're on track or not. Break it down into smaller tasks. A good range is 4 to 40 hours per task, with the majority of around 8 hours.

To see which tasks that are allocated to a specific team member, filter the board by clicking on the **All** link in the upper-right corner and then select that member. You can also group the entire board by team members.

> **Always keep Remaining Work updated**
>
> The **Remaining Work** field is central to make the burn-down graph and planning work. As a scrum master for your team, coach everyone to keep this updated. Never think about the past, always update with the value you feel is right TODAY.

There is a corresponding Kanban board, which is also very useful to get an overview of the state of the product backlog items.

5 – Build automation

Next to source control, the most important part in getting a continuous integration process working is build automation.

TFS 2012 Build is an end-to-end build automation engine for orchestrating the build process.

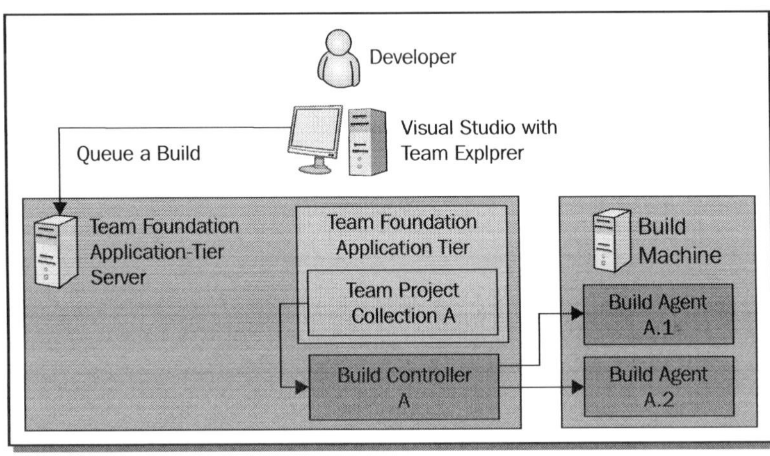

The two components of TFS Build are the **Build Controller** and the **Build Agent**. These are services running on one or multiple servers. Each build controller is registered with a single team project collection, and receives the request when a build is triggered. The build controller then queues the build on a suitable build agent.

> **Place the build controller on the TFS server**
>
> The build controller distributes a build to any available build agent on any build machine. By placing your build controller on the TFS server, and NOT on one of the build machines, you can avoid making any build machine a critical point of failure.

Creating a build definition

To create a build definition in TFS 2012, follow these steps:

1. In **Team Explorer**, click on the **New Build Definition** link on the **Builds** hub.
2. **General**: Enter a name for the build definition in a manner similar to the following: <Product>.<Branch>.<Trigger>. For example, MyApplication.Dev.CI.
3. **Trigger**: The trigger determines how the build should start.
    - **Manual**: The build must be triggered manually by a team member.
    - **Continuous Integration (CI)**: The build will start automatically when a check-in occurs inside the workspace of the build.
    - **Rolling Builds**: Accumulate check-ins until the prior build finishes. You also have the option to define a fixed interval. If you set it to 15 minutes, the build will start at most every 15 minutes.

> **Prefer continuous integration to rolling builds**
>
> Only use rolling builds when you are out of build resources. A rolling build will reduce your build granularity, and make it more difficult to see what causes a build to fail.

- **Gated check-in**: A **gated check-in** is similar to a CI build, but with the difference that the check-in will only be accepted if the builds runs successfully. Larger and/or distributed teams can sometimes end up in a situation where the builds keep failing and no-one manages to get it back to the working stage again. A gated check-in build makes sure that no one can check in something that breaks the build.

> **Use gated check-in in non-ideal situations**
>
> In a non-ideal world, teams do not always communicate as well as you would like them to. Especially when the teams are distributed globally, this can be a challenge. A broken build will then cause more pain than you can accept, and the pain killer is the gated check-in. However, if you can improve team communication, prefer that over a gated check-in.

For more information on gated check-in builds, see http://msdn.microsoft.com/en-us/library/dd787631(v=vs.110).aspx.

- **Schedule**: Used for daily/nightly builds that should run once every day.

4. **Workspace**: Here, you define the workspace for the build. It is very important to make the workspace as small as possible, otherwise the build will download a lot of unnecessary source code every time the build runs.

5. **Build Default**: This specifies which build controller should handle the build.

   You also define the `Drop` folder path here. This must be a server share where the build service account has read/write permissions. The recommended drop path is `\\<Server>\<Share>\<TeamProject>\<Project>\<Trigger>`, for example: `\\server\drop\eBook\SampleApplication\CI`.

6. **Process**: Configure what the build should do. First of all, you must select which build process template should be used. By default, you have three different templates to choose from:

   - **DefaultTemplate11.X.xaml**: This is the standard template that you should use for most build definitions. It also serves as the basis for customizations. It implements a full end-to-end build with label, compile, analyze, test, copy to drop, report, and notification.
   - **UpgradeTemplate.xaml**: This is used for build definitions that were upgraded from earlier versions of TFS 2005 and 2008. It is a minimal workflow template that launches **MSBuild** to execute a MSBuild project file. Use this as a temporary solution until you have converted your older builds to TFS 2012.
   - **LabDefaultTemplate.11.xaml**: This is used for builds that implement a full **Build-Deploy-Test** (BDT) workflow. This is related to **lab management,** where you want to deploy the build to one or more virtual or physical machines and then perform tests on those machines as a part of the build.

   For more information on this topic, see `http://msdn.microsoft.com/en-us/library/ee471614(v=vs.110).aspx`.

   Select **DefaultTemplate.11.X.xaml**. Now, you need to define the build process parameters for this build definition:

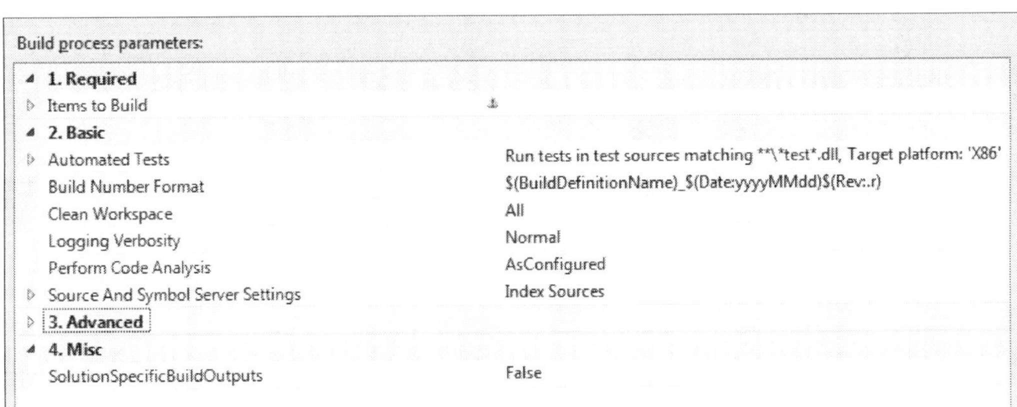

7. The only required parameter is **Items to Build**. This is the path to one or more projects/solutions in source control that should be built. You can also configure the configuration(s), such as **Debug | Any CPU,** for example.

The rest of the parameters have default values, which do not require any extra input, but you will want to learn what these are and what they do. You can, for example, configure log verbosity, the format of the build number, which build agent should be selected for the build, and so on.

8. **Retention Policy**: On the last tab, you can configure how many builds of each outcome should be stored. This is to avoid the drop folders and the TFS database to grow too much. For each outcome, you can configure what should be deleted.

You are done; save the build definition.

Running a build

To run a build manually, right-click on the build definition in Team Explorer and select **Queue New Build**.

This brings up the **Queue Build** dialog box, where you can override several build settings and parameters for this build before starting it. The CI, Rolling, or Gated Check-in builds will start automatically when you check in. The queued build shows up under the **My Builds** section in the **Builds** hub. Double-click on it to see the build summary:

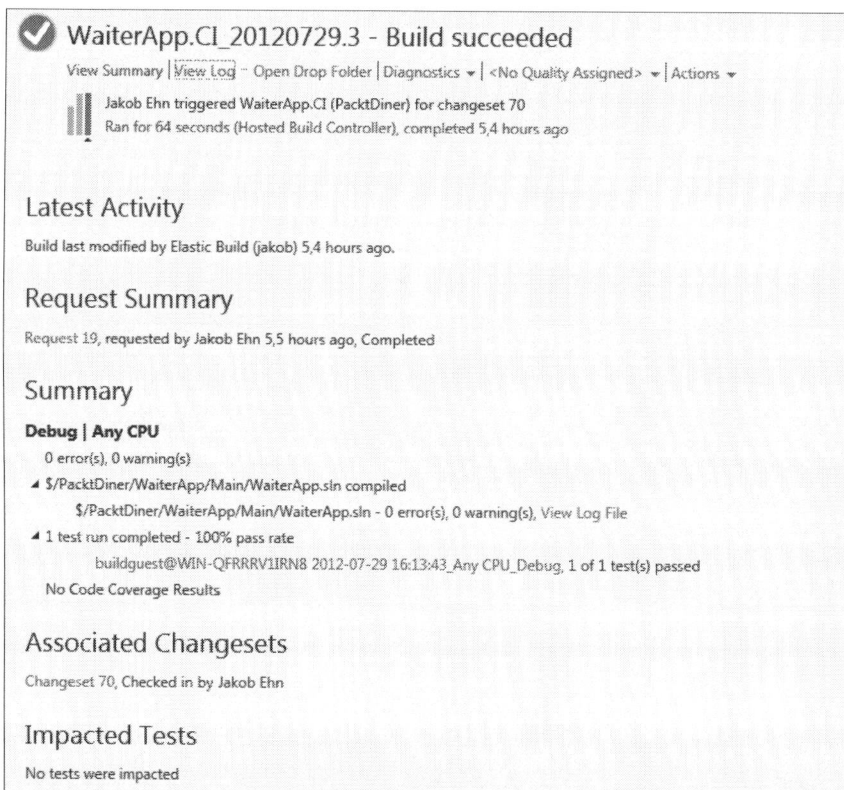

The build summary shows all the relevant information of the build, with links to the complete log and drop folders where you can access the output from the build.

Customizing build definitions

You will eventually need to modify the build workflow, for example, if you want to copy the build output to a specific location. For guidance and best practices on build customization, see the *Visual Studio ALM Rangers guidance* for how to do that at `http://vsarbuildguide.codeplex.com/`.

People and places you should get to know

If you need help with Team Foundation Server 2012, here are some people and places which will prove invaluable:

Official Sites

- **Visual Studio Homepage**: `http://www.microsoft.com/visualstudio/en-us`
- **Team Foundation Server on Channel 9, useful videos**: `http://channel9.msdn.com/Tags/team+foundation+server`
- **Visual Studio ALM and Team Foundation Server Blog**: `http://blogs.msdn.com/b/visualstudioalm/`
- **All the extensions you need, find them on the Visual Studio Gallery**: `http://visualstudiogallery.msdn.microsoft.com/`
- **ALM Overview**: `http://www.microsoft.com/visualstudio/eng/alm/overview`

Articles and tutorials

- **Customizing Team Build, blog series by Ewald Hofman**: `http://www.ewaldhofman.nl/post/2010/04/20/Customize-Team-Build-2010-e28093-Part-1-Introduction.aspx`
- **Guidance on using friendly DNS names in your TFS environment**: `http://www.edsquared.com/2011/01/03/Using+Friendly+DNS+Names+In+Your+TFS+Environment.aspx`

Community

- **Visual Studio ALM Rangers**: `http://msdn.microsoft.com/en-us/vstudio/ee358787.aspx`
- **Visual Studio Team Foundation Server Forums**: `http://social.msdn.microsoft.com/Forums/en-US/category/vstfs`
- **StackOverflow TFS**: `http://stackoverflow.com/questions/tagged/tfs`
- **Radio TFS**: A great podcast around Visual Studio and TFS: `http://www.radiotfs.com/`
- **Community TFS Build Extensions**: `http://tfsbuildextensions.codeplex.com/`

Blogs

- **Brian Harry, Product Unit Manager for TFS**: `http://blogs.msdn.com/b/bharry/`
- **Brian Keller, Microsoft Sr. Technical Evangelist for Visual Studio ALM**: `http: //blogs.msdn.com/b/briankel/`
- **Ed Blankenship, Program Manager Visual Studio Testing & Lab Management**: `http://www.edsquared.com/`
- **Martin Hinshelwood, Senior ALM Consultant and ALM MVP**: This blog contains tons of useful guidance around Visual Studio and TFS – `http://blog.hinshelwood.com/`
- **Neno Loje, a leading German author and ALM MVP**: `http://msmvps.com/blogs/vstsblog/`
- **Marcel de Vries, Dutch speaker and ALM MVP**: `http://blogs.infosupport.com/author/marcelv/`
- **Adam Cogan, ALM MVP, speaker and Regional MS Technical Director for Austrialia**: `http://www.adamcogan.com/`
- **Jeff Levinson, ALM MVP and author**: `http://blog.nwcadence.com/author/jefflevinson/`
- **Tarun Arora, ALM MVP, active blogger and ALM MVP**: `http://geekswithblogs.net/tarunarora/Default.aspx`
- **Martin Woodward, Program Manager Visual Studio Team Explorer Everywhere**: `http://www.woodwardweb.com/`
- **Ricci Gian Maria, ALM MVP, active blogger**: `http://www.codewrecks.com/blog/`

Third-party tools

- **Urban Turtle Agile/Scrum Management Tools for TFS**: `http://urbanturtle.com/`
- **TeamPulse Agile Project Management Tools**: `http://www.telerik.com/agile-project-management-tools/`
- **InRelease – Agile Release Management for TFS**: `http://www.inreleasesoftware.com/`
- **inteGREAT Requirement Management Tools for TFS**: `http://www.edevtech.com/products.html`

Other Books

See the following books for diving deeper into the TFS:

- **Professional Application Lifecycle Management**: `http://www.amazon.com/gp/product/1118314085`
- **Professional Team Foundation Server**: `http://www.amazon.com/gp/product/1118314093`
- **Software Testing with Visual Studio 2010**: `http://www.amazon.com/dp/0321734483`
- **Agile Software Engineering with Visual Studio**: `http://www.amazon.com/Agile-Software-Engineering-Visual-Studio/dp/0321685857`
- **Pro Application Lifecycle Management with Visual Studio 2012**: `http://www.amazon.com/Application-Lifecycle-Management-Visual-Professional/dp/1430243449`

Extensions

- A list of useful extensions can be found at `http://geekswithblogs.net/terje/archive/2012/03/22/visual-studio-amp-tfs-11-ndash-list-of-extensions-and.aspx`
- The Visual Studio Team Foundation Server Power Tools is very useful for all who use TFS 2012: `http://visualstudiogallery.msdn.microsoft.com/27832337-62ae-4b54-9b00-98bb4fb7041a`

Twitter

- Follow Microsoft's Jason Zander on Twitter: `http://twitter.com/#!/jlzander`
- Follow ALM MVP and ALM Ranger Build Guide Lead Mike Fourie at `http://twitter.com/#!/MikeFourie`
- Follow Willy-Peter Schaub, Microsoft ALM Ranger at `http://twitter.com/#!/wpschaub`
- For more open source information, follow Packt at `http://twitter.com/#!/packtopensource`

[PACKT] enterprise
professional expertise distilled
PUBLISHING

Thank you for buying

Team Foundation Server 2012 Starter

About Packt Publishing

Packt, pronounced 'packed', published its first book "Mastering phpMyAdmin for Effective MySQL Management" in April 2004 and subsequently continued to specialize in publishing highly focused books on specific technologies and solutions.

Our books and publications share the experiences of your fellow IT professionals in adapting and customizing today's systems, applications, and frameworks. Our solution based books give you the knowledge and power to customize the software and technologies you're using to get the job done. Packt books are more specific and less general than the IT books you have seen in the past. Our unique business model allows us to bring you more focused information, giving you more of what you need to know, and less of what you don't.

Packt is a modern, yet unique publishing company, which focuses on producing quality, cutting-edge books for communities of developers, administrators, and newbies alike. For more information, please visit our website: `www.packtpub.com`.

About Packt Enterprise

In 2010, Packt launched two new brands, Packt Enterprise and Packt Open Source, in order to continue its focus on specialization. This book is part of the Packt Enterprise brand, home to books published on enterprise software – software created by major vendors, including (but not limited to) IBM, Microsoft and Oracle, often for use in other corporations. Its titles will offer information relevant to a range of users of this software, including administrators, developers, architects, and end users.

Writing for Packt

We welcome all inquiries from people who are interested in authoring. Book proposals should be sent to author@packtpub.com. If your book idea is still at an early stage and you would like to discuss it first before writing a formal book proposal, contact us; one of our commissioning editors will get in touch with you.

We're not just looking for published authors; if you have strong technical skills but no writing experience, our experienced editors can help you develop a writing career, or simply get some additional reward for your expertise.

[PACKT] enterprise
PUBLISHING
professional expertise distilled

Visual Studio 2012 Cookbook

ISBN: 978-1-84968-652-5 Paperback: 272 pages

50 simple but incredibly effective recipes to immediately get you working with the exciting features of Visual Studio 2012

1. Take advantage of all of the new features of Visual Studio 2012, no matter what your programming language specialty is!
2. Get to grips with Windows 8 Store App development, .NET 4.5, asynchronous coding and new team development changes in this book and e-book
3. A concise and practical First Look Cookbook to immediately get you coding with Visual Studio 2012

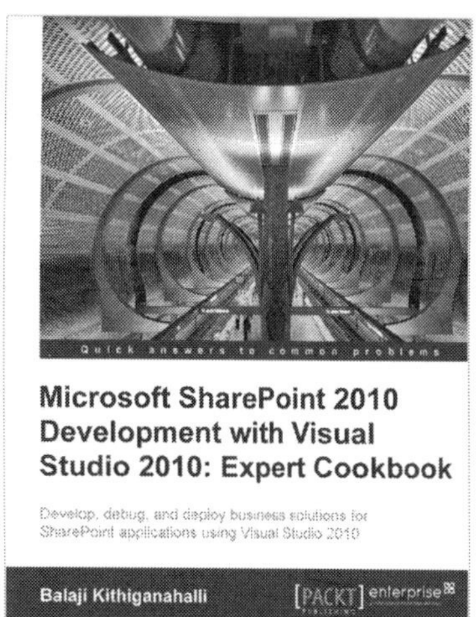

Microsoft SharePoint 2010 Development with Visual Studio 2010 Expert Cookbook

ISBN: 978-1-84968-458-3 Paperback: 296 pages

Develop, debug, and deploy business solutions for SharePoint applications using Visual Studio 2010

1. A step-by-step guide for brand-new Office Create applications using the latest client object model and create custom web services for your SharePoint environment with this book and ebook.
2. Full of illustrations, diagrams and key points for debugging and deploying your solutions securely to the SharePoint environment.
3. Recipes with step-by-step instructions with detailed explanation on how each recipe works and working code examples

Please check **www.PacktPub.com** for information on our titles

[PACKT] enterprise
professional expertise distilled
PUBLISHING

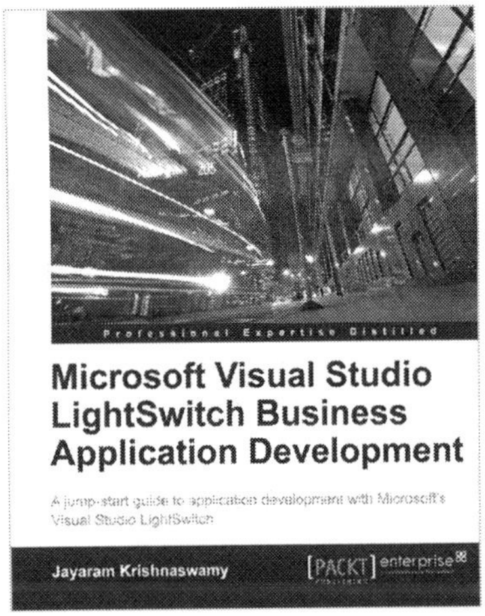

Microsoft Visual Studio LightSwitch Business Application Development

ISBN: 978-1-84968-286-2 Paperback: 384 pages

A jump-start guide to application development with Microsoft's Visual Studio LightSwitch

1. A hands-on guide, packed with screenshots and step-by-step instructions and relevant background information—making it easy to build your own application with this book and ebook
2. Easily connect to various data sources with practical examples and easy-to-follow instructions
3. Create entities and screens both from scratch and using built-in templates

---

Microsoft Dynamics CRM 2011: Dashboards Cookbook

ISBN: 978-1-84968-440-8 Paperback: 266 pages

Over 50 simple but incredibly effective recipes for creating customizing, and interacting with rich dashboards and charts

1. Take advantage of all of the latest Dynamics CRM dashboard features for visualizing your most important data at a glance.
2. Understand how iFrames, chart customizations, advanced WebResources and more can improve your dashboards in Dynamics CRM by using this book and eBook.
3. A highly practical cookbook bursting with a range of exciting task-based recipes for mastering Microsoft Dynamics CRM 2011 Dashboards.

Please check **www.PacktPub.com** for information on our titles

29982100R00042

Made in the USA
Lexington, KY
20 February 2014